JESUS AND FIRST-CENTURY CHRISTIANITY IN JERUSALEM

Elizabeth McNamer

and

Bargil Pixner

Paulist Press
New York/Mahwah, NJ

Nihil Obstat: +Most Reverend Anthony M. Milone, DD
        Diocese of Great Falls-Billings
        Censor Librorum
Imprimatur: +Most Reverend Anthony M. Milone, DD
        Bishop of Great Falls-Billings

Cover design by Joy Taylor
Book design by Lynn Else
Photo credits: The photographs and maps used in this book are either from the author's collection or taken from the Paulist Press collection.

The financial contribution of the late Fr. Bargil Pixner's family toward the publication of this book is gratefully acknowledged.

Library of Congress Cataloging-in-Publication Data

McNamer, Elizabeth Mary.
  Jesus and first-century Christianity in Jerusalem / Elizabeth McNamer and Bargil Pixner.
    p. cm.
  ISBN-13: 978-0-8091-4523-2 (alk. paper)
  1. Church history—Primitive and early church, ca. 30–600. 2. Jerusalem—Church history. I. Pixner, Bargil. II. Title.
  BR162.3.M425 2008
  275.694'4201—dc22

                                                2008002479

Published by Paulist Press
997 Macarthur Boulevard
Mahwah, New Jersey 07430

www.paulistpress.com

Printed and bound in Mexico

CONTENTS

List of Illustrations   v

Preface   vii

Prologue: The Background of Jesus: The Essenes, the Nazoreans,
            and Jesus' Immediate Family   1

Chapter 1: The Events after the Resurrection: The Years 30–40   13

Chapter 2: Community Life, Tensions, the Council of Jerusalem:
            The Years 40–50   32

Chapter 3: Problems Adapting to Gentiles: The Years 50–60   44

Chapter 4: Death of James, Heresy, Flight to Pella:
            The Years 60–70   55

Chapter 5: Return to Jerusalem: The Years 70–80   65

Chapter 6: Writings, Liturgy, Hierarchy: The Years 80–100   77

Chapter 7: Rebellions, Persecution, and Division:
            The Years 100–135   86

Epilogue   96

Works Cited   98

Paulist Press gratefully acknowledges the generous financial contribution toward the publication of this book made by Fr. Pixner's brother and sisters, Maria, Alois, Elisabeth, and Anna Maria, in loving memory of the book's coauthor, Rev. Bargil Pixner.

LIST OF ILLUSTRATIONS

PHOTOGRAPHS

The Essene gate, pg. vii

Ritual bath at Qumran, pg. 1

Qumran cave in which the first Dead Sea Scrolls were found, pg. 2

Gamala, a fortified town founded by Hasmonean ruler Alexander Jannaeus, which harbored many Zealots, pg. 3

The Mount of Olives and Gethsemane, pg. 8

Overview of Jerusalem, pg. 11

Countryside near Nazareth, pg. 14

The ancient synagogue at Capernaum, pg. 19

Mikvah, or Essene ritual bath, pg. 22

Tomb of Jesus, pg. 25

Theater at Sepphoris, an important Greco-Roman town near Nazareth, pg. 32

Agrippa's palace at Caesarea Philippi, pg. 35

Icon of the Dormition (death or "falling asleep") of Mary, pg. 42

Model of Jerusalem Temple: Entrance of the Holy of Holies, pg. 45

Church of St. Peter in Gallicantu ("Cock Crow") and steps to house of Caiaphas, where Jesus may have walked, pg. 46

Bethsaida, pg. 55

Pinnacle of the Temple, pg. 57

The Ossuary of St. James?, pg. 58

Stairs to the Temple Mount, pg. 60

Dormition Abbey, pg. 63

Masada, Jewish fortress that fell to Rome in 73 CE, pg. 67

Synagogue wall under Cenacle, pg. 70

The Citadel, which protected Jerusalem for many centuries because of its location high on a hill, pg. 72

Model of Jerusalem, section, pg. 73

Herod's palace at Masada, pg. 77

Remains of temple to Livia Julia (wife of Augustus), built by Philip Herod in 30 CE, pg. 79

Steps leading up to Herodian palace, pg. 80

Seal of Solomon on the ancient synagogue at Capernaum, pg. 83

Beth Shean, head city of the Decapolis, pg. 86

Sea of Galilee, pg. 90

Icon of the Resurrection, pg. 93

Mosaic in the church at Tabgha, traditional site of the multiplication of the loaves and fishes, pg. 94

Casting a net on the Sea of Galilee, pg. 97

MAPS

Essene Quarter, pg. 16

Herodian Jerusalem, pg. 28

The Roman Empire, pg. 34

The land of Jesus, pg. 39

Paul's missionary journeys, pg. 50

Palestine under early procurators, pg. 53

PREFACE

Church history, in general, gives little prominence to the community that was formed in Jerusalem on Mount Zion and from which the message of Jesus went out to all the world. The gentile church of Paul, which was to guide the development of Western civilization, has overshadowed all else. Jewish Christianity, on the other hand, has been marginalized, even regarded as heretical. Only since the discovery of the Dead Sea Scrolls in 1947 have we become aware of the diversity within Judaism at the time of Jesus, and since the coincidental creation of the state of Israel that attention has been paid to the Jewish origins of Christianity.

In 1977 Father Bargil Pixner, along with Dr. Doron Chen, undertook an excavation close to Mount Zion of an ancient city wall that contained a gate. They established that the wall and gate date to the first century and the gate fits exactly that mentioned by Josephus as the "gate of the Essenes."

The Essene gate

Much scholarly research in the years since has focused on the Essene gate. It is the closest entry in the city that leads to the area of the Cenacle (the upper room) believed to be the place of the first Christian community in Jerusalem. Scholars now agree that a community of Essenes occupied this site during the first century of the Common Era. Many are making a connection between this group and the early followers of Jesus.

I joined Father Pixner in his research in 1994 as a result of my involvement in the archaeological excavations at Bethsaida and their connections with the origins of Christianity.

We believe that it was in the guest house adjoining the Essene quarter that Jesus had the Last Supper. It was here that he appeared to his disciples on Easter Sunday, and it was here that the descent of the Holy Spirit occurred on Pentecost. It was here that the first Christian community established itself under the leadership of the family of Jesus, who were known as Nazoreans. This was the beginning of Jewish Christianity in Jerusalem.

Using the discovery of the Essene gate and the hypotheses given above as our base, we have looked to the Acts of the Apostles as our main source. The possibility of an Essene connection illuminates several events in the Acts, such as the time and place of the Pentecost event, the source of the community of goods, and the priests mentioned in Acts 6:7. We believe that those priests were Essene.

Looking to the writings of Hegesippus (quoted by Eusebius) and Josephus, we have concluded that one of those Essene converts was a certain Thabuti, who played a major role during the time of the bishopric of James, the brother of Jesus. (Several other scholars have hypothesized this also.) He had expected to be elected bishop after the death of James in 62. We argue that it was he who led the first dissent in the church, which was the Ebionite heresy. As with other groups in Judaism, this was not a complete break. The Ebionites and the Nazoreans differed in their idea of the nature of Christ but nonetheless lived side by side. There was room for flexibility of opinions in the early church. (This lasted until 150, when heresy was first defined.) In 66, at the time of the Roman-Jewish war, many Christians fled to Pella. Some Ebionites seem to have stayed in Jerusalem. Even much later, Epiphanius tells us, Nazoreans and Ebionites lived together in the Batanea.

We also believe that the Nazoreans returned to Mount Zion, as mentioned in Eusebius, during the reign of the Emperor Vespasian, probably around the year 74. They built a synagogue and regarded themselves as Jews. While Sadducees and Essenes faded out after the destruction of the Temple, the Pharisees became the main bearers of Judaism and the contrast between them and the Judean Christians became sharper with time. We believe that up until the end of the Bar Kokhba war in 136 CE, the Jewish Christians considered themselves within Judaism. The split came only when they refused to accept the messianic claim of Bar Kokhba, a claim that, incidentally, was endorsed by the prominent rabbi Aqiba.

After the Bar Kokhba war, the Romans forbade the Jews access to Jerusalem. We are not sure how this ban affected the Jewish Christians. Since they had not supported the rebellion, they may have been permitted to stay. If so, they were certainly reduced to a very small number. The line of Jewish bishops, all of whom were Jewish and connected to the family of Jesus, stopped in the year 135. A Gentile bishop, Mark, was then appointed. The Jewish community probably accepted him, while continuing to exercise their own Jewish heritage.

The community continued a precarious and quasi-autonomous existence up to the end of the fourth century. They built a wall around Mount Zion at the time of Emperor Heliogabaldus in 220. In the fifth century, they were absorbed into the Imperial church of the Byzantine Empire.

Some of our conclusions are speculative, but we hope they are a basis for further studies on the beginnings of Christianity.

This book is intended for a general readership. Although we have done the scholarly research required, we have avoided encumbering the story with footnotes.

A major source for this study is the evidence of the archaeology of Mount Zion. As we shall see, the stones will cry out! We have used the Acts of the Apostles and the other books of the New Testament, the Old Testament, Josephus, Philo, Hegesippus, Eusebius, Epiphanius, the *Odes of Solomon*, the Dead Sea Scrolls, the Talmud, and some of the extrabiblical literature, such as the *Protoevangelium of James*, the *Martyrdom and Ascension of Isaiah*, the *Genesis Apocryphon*, and the Clementine Letters.

We have consulted with some of the modern scholars of early Christianity: Etienne Nodet, Justin Taylor, Emile Puech, Brian J. Capper, and Rainer Riesner. We have used also as sources R.E. Brown, J.H. Charlesworth, A. Jaubert, E. Ruckstuhl, H.J. Schoeps, Y. Yadin, A. Harnack, R. Bultmann, D. Chaen, D. Baldi, B. Baggati, R. Arav, D. Flusser, R. Freund, W. Horbury, and others.

Bargil Pixner
Elizabeth McNamer
Mount Zion
Jerusalem

THE BACKGROUND OF JESUS: THE ESSENES, THE NAZOREANS, AND JESUS' IMMEDIATE FAMILY

The Essene Connection

Many sects of Judaism existed in Palestine during the lifetime of Jesus, each with its own interpretation of the Torah (the Law). The three main sects were the Sadducees, the Essenes (The Devout Ones), and the Pharisees. We know this from the writings of Flavius Josephus, a Jewish historian of the first century, who claims to have belonged to all three sects at various times during his life. The core of the first two consisted of priests *(Kohanim)*, while the Pharisees were, to a large extent, laypeople. The Sadducees were found only in Jerusalem. Essenes were in many villages about the country but also grouped together in communities in Qumran, Batanea, and Mount Zion. The Pharisees operated everywhere.

The origin of the Essenes goes back to the election of the Maccabees in 180 BCE. We read in 1 Macc 2:29: "Many who were seeking

Ritual bath at Qumran

righteousness and justice went down to the wilderness to dwell there." They fought alongside Matthias Maccabee and his troops: "Then there united with them a company of Hasideans, mighty warriors of Israel, every one who offered himself willingly for the law." (1 Macc 2:42). With the Essenes' help the Maccabees, who later assumed the dynastic name Hasmonean, won the war.

Although the Essenes had been enthusiastic supporters of the Hasmonean-Maccabees against the Greek might of Syria, they vehemently objected when Jonathan, who already held the office of king, assumed the office of high priest as well in 152 BCE. (He may have wanted access to the treasury of the Temple to pay off his soldiers.) Essene priests claimed to be the sons of Zadok, the chief priest of David's son, Solomon, and as such felt that they were the legitimate heirs to the High Priesthood of the Temple. Simon, who was the current high priest at the time of Jonathan, declared the sacrificial offering in the Temple to be illegitimate. He and his followers went off to the desert to await the coming of the Messiah. This Simon is thought to be the one referred to as the Teacher of Righteousness in the Dead Sea Scrolls.

Qumran cave in which the first Dead Sea Scrolls were found

Since the Essenes did not have access to the Temple, this devout group substituted ritual cleansing in the *mikvot* (ritual bathhouse) for sacrifice. Scandalized by the Hasmonean priesthood's adoption of a feast-calendar based on the Babylonian lunar system, they created their own calendar based on the solar cycle. Their year had 364 days or fifty-two weeks. Aware, of course, that they shorted themselves a day, they made up for this by adding a week every seven years. In the Genesis account of creation, the sun was created on the fourth day, Wednesday, so the Essene calendar celebrated Rosh Hashanah (feast of the creation of the world) on a Wednesday. The first day of the month fell on a Wednesday, as did the fifteenth. Since Passover (*Pesach*) was celebrated on the fifteenth of the first month, this important festival was always celebrated on a Wednesday. So also Tabernacles (*Sukkoth*) was celebrated on a Wednesday. It must be remembered, however, that because the day was measured from sundown to sundown, Wednesday would have commenced the evening before. In the opinion of some scholars (Annie Jaubert and S. Talmon), this solar calendar seems to have been the ancient calendar of Israel during the pre-Babylonian period, and the lunar calendar with its Babylonian designation of the months Nisan, Iyyar, Sivan, Tammoz,

Gamala, a fortified town founded by Hasmonean ruler Alexander Jannaeus, which harbored many Zealots

Ab, Elul, Tishri, Kslev, Tebet, Shebat, and Adar was a later adaptation to the universal calendar of that epoch.

The Nazoreans

At the beginning of the first century BCE, the Hasmonean Alexander Jannaeus conquered Galilee (Josephus, *Antiquities* 12:393ff). Gentiles were settled in the valleys of this fertile land (the mountains were unpopulated) after the Assyrian wars of the eighth century BCE. Isaiah called it "Galilee of the Gentiles." Because Alexander Jannaeus wanted to make Galilee Jewish and forced circumcision on the population, many left and immigrated to the Decapolis (the ten pagan cities on the other side of the Jordan River). At this time, Jews still living in Babylon since the deportation in the sixth century were invited to return.

Several scholars suggest that among the returnees were the Nazoreans, a clan who claimed to be descendants of David, to whom the family of Jesus belonged. These people derived their name from the word *Netzer* (Isa 11:1), "shoot of," Jesse, and regarded themselves as the royal family from whom the Messiah would come. Eusebius, quoting Julius Africanus, who wrote in the second century, informs us that the Nazoreans of the family of Jesus came originally from the villages of Kochaba and Nazara:

Few in antiquity have thought it worthwhile leaving personal memoirs, in that they had records or drew the names from memory or from some other archival material, in order to preserve the memory of their noble birth. But among them were the already mentioned "Desposynoi" (Lord's people) so called because of their relationship with the Savior's family. Originating from the Jewish villages of Nazara and Kochaba, they spread out over the rest of the country. (Eusebius, *Ecclesiastical History* 1.7.14 PG 94, 97/99)

These two villages bear suspiciously messianic names, Kochaba meaning "village of the star" and Nazareth "village of the shoot." Genealogies were of great importance in establishing identity (Ezra 2:62–63). Since the Messiah was expected, lines had to be kept pure. The Davidic families in the Babylonian Diaspora would certainly have kept track of their genealogies; two are preserved in the gospels of Matthew (1:1–16) and Luke (3:23–38).

This remnant of the tribe of Jesse returned to take up a new life in their ancient homeland. Some settled in the Batanea near the Yarmuk River at the village of Kochaba, east of the Sea of Galilee. Others of the tribe settled in a little hillside village in the Galilee, which they named Nazareth from their tribal name. Archaeological excavations conducted by Father Bellarmino Bagatti between 1955 and 1970 have established that this Nazarean village was not occupied after the Assyrian conquest of the eighth century until some eighty years or so before the Common Era.

Was the family of Jesus who lived in Nazareth influenced by Essenism? Several scholars, including J.H. Charlesworth, think that this was so. We indeed have indications that they might have been. Josephus and Philo say that the Essenes (variously known as the Devout Ones, the Pious Ones, or the Hasidim) lived in many villages throughout the land. Julius Africanus tells us that Essenes were well established in the Batanea. (Batanea is referred to as the "land of Damascus" in the scrolls.)

Jesus' Immediate Family

The apocryphal *Protoevangelium of James* claims that Mary was born in Jerusalem (near the Bethesda pool), spent her early years serving in the Temple, and took a vow of virginity at an early age. Joachim, the father of Mary, chose a man to take care of her who would respect that vow. The taking of this vow seems to have been an Essene practice. The Temple scroll from Qumran says: "If a woman has taken a vow or binds herself with a formal pledge, in the house of her father, with an oath, in her youth and her father hears the vow, the formal pledge with which she bound herself will remain in force." It would not have been uncommon for a widower with children to take as a wife one who was to remain a virgin. The Gospels tell us that Jesus grew up in a large family. The names of his brothers are given as James, Jude, Simon, and Joseph. He had two sisters whose names are given in apocryphal literature as Salome and Mary. Roman Catholic tradition, stemming from Saint Jerome, speaks of these as "cousins," but Orthodox tradition says that they were children of Joseph by a former marriage.

Jesus' family were devout, law-oriented Jews. Luke tells us that they went every year to Jerusalem for the celebration of the Passover. John says that they went for other celebrations as well, and we can infer from John 7:5–10 that they celebrated the festivals according to the Essene calendar. They were convinced that they were of the Davidic line. They kept the Torah, fulfilling "everything required by the law of the Lord" (Luke 2:39), as did the Essenes. It is indeed possible that even if they were not themselves Essenes they were influenced by this sect and that Jesus grew up under Essene idealism.

Jesus may have had a life-changing experience when he went to the Jordan near Jericho and was baptized by John the Baptist. He was singled out by a voice saying "This is my beloved son."

John's father, Zechariah, was a priest of the division of Abijah. (There were twenty-four divisions of priests.) Luke relates that John "was in the wilderness until the day he appeared publicly to Israel" (Luke 1: 80). It was the custom at Qumran to take in children at an early age and train them for their later vocation, and some believe that John was raised by Essenes at Qumran. It was not unusual for preachers to go to the desert and to move about from one place to another. John may have been raised in the core of this sect, but then received a mission to preach to all of the people and left the Qumran community. If he did so he would, according to Josephus, be still bound by his oaths as an Essene. Josephus also tells us that people who left the Essenes often died of starvation because they did not find food that was allowed. We are told in the Gospel of Matthew that John ate locusts and wild honey and wore a garment of camel's hair with a leather belt (the clothing of a prophet, especially Elijah).

John declared: "Prepare the way of the Lord, make his paths straight" (Matt 3:3).

This passage is found in the Community Rule of the Essenes: "In the desert, prepare the way of the Lord. Straighten in the steppe a roadway for our God."

Like the Essenes, John offered a baptism of repentance, but while the Essenes baptized themselves continually, John's baptism seems to have been one of initiation.

One of the places at which he baptized was in Bethany "beyond the Jordan," which was in Batanea at the Yarmuk River. This was on the pilgrim route over which the Jews of Babylon passed on their way to the feast of Passover. It was also the place where the horses were trained for the army of Herod Philip. Luke reports that many came to be baptized by John, including soldiers who seem to have had great regard for John. Later, when Herod Antipas, John's executioner, inherited his brother's territory, he used these soldiers to fight against his former father-in-law. They deserted.

After his baptism by John, and the voice from heaven, Jesus went on a forty-day retreat into the desert, meditating on the meaning of the voice. He overcame the temptation of playing the messianic role suggested by Satan. Then he went once more back to the Baptist.

There, Jesus met the fishermen of Bethsaida, who also had come to see and listen to John the Baptist. John, an itinerant preacher, later moved on to Ainon near Salim (John 3:23).

The public ministry of Jesus probably started in the spring of 28 CE and lasted for less than three years.

One of the defining events in the life of Jesus was the cleansing of the Temple. John's Gospel gives this as happening early in his ministry, possible around the year 28. After it, "many believed in his name" (John 2:23). The Essenes had a community in Jerusalem and deplored the sacrifices of the Temple. It may be that Essene priests became believers after watching this incident. They might have seen in Jesus the potential Messiah. Messianic expectations were well established among the Essenes. William Horbury, who has studied the scrolls extensively, says that the Essenes expected a messiah who would be human but endowed with superhuman qualities, including preexistence, and might even be thought of as divine.

Jesus, however, had already decided to leave the narrow confines of their idealism. His mission was to all of Israel. The Essenes, although extremely pious, were not made for him. He had to remain open to all.

When John was put into prison by Herod Antipas, Jesus left Judea and went through Samaria back to Galilee (John 4:45). The village of Nazareth had no more than 150 inhabitants, but they did possess a synagogue. Since the Nazoreans drew their name from Isaiah 11:1 (shoot of Jesse), the prophet Isaiah had a prominent place in their synagogue readings. It was from Isaiah that Jesus read when he first revealed himself:

"The Spirit of the Lord is upon me,
because he has anointed me
    to bring good news to the poor.
He has sent me to proclaim release to the captives
    and recovery of sight to the blind,
    to let the oppressed go free,
to proclaim the year of the Lord's favor." (Luke 4:18–19)

When Jesus came to Galilee, his clan received him with jubilation because they also had seen the great things he had done in Jerusalem during the Paschal feast. They too had been present at the scene. Was he the expected Messiah, one of their own? Jesus, although sensitive to the ideology of his family and his countrymen, knew that their philosophy was not suited to his mission. Jesus shocked and angered them by his words "a prophet has no honor in the prophet's own country" (John 4:44), so much so that the townspeople tried to throw him over a cliff.

Jesus left his village behind and went down to the lake at Capernaum. There he met the men who had become his friends and who had been influenced by John. The first four disciples were from Bethsaida. Bethsaida was located close to the land of the gentiles, the Decapolis. Archeological evidence suggests this small town had a mixed population. Greek and Aramaic were spoken here, and it was under the jurisdiction of Philip Herod, who was Roman in sympathy. These people were more open than those at Nazareth.

Jesus deliberately chose people from that wedge between the Jewish Galilee and the pagan Decapolis. He did not choose the core of his followers from the pious, but from the more worldly. Jesus had to be open to the general public and could not be restricted. There would be a dichotomy between his family and his new friends all during his public ministry.

Jesus made his headquarters at Capernaum with his new disciples. His public ministry in Galilee was largely centered around the "evangelical triangle," Capernaum, Bethsaida, and Chorazim, with occasional forays to gentile territory. His family kept aloof from him and his *haburah* (circle of friends). Mark's Gospel bluntly tells us of the incident when Mary and his brothers went to Capernaum to fetch him home: "And looking at those who sat around him, he said, 'Here are my mother and my brothers!'" (Mark 3:34).

Jesus celebrated the feast of Hanukkah in Jerusalem in 29 CE, a feast that the Essenes did not celebrate. This feast had been introduced by the Hasmonean dynasty in memory of the cleansing and rededication of the Temple that had been desecrated by the Syrians. This is further evidence that Jesus himself was not an Essene.

Bethany

There are two places called Bethany. One is beyond the Jordan, which is a region where Jesus first encountered the fishermen who had come from Bethsaida to meet John the Baptist (the region of Batanea). In some of the Targums (Greek translations to Aramaic), the Batanea is referred to as Bethany (John 10:40). The other Bethany was situated on the eastern slope of the Mount of Olives, one-and-a-half kilometers from Jerusalem, and was where Jesus withdrew after a mob tried to stone him in the Temple (John 10:31).

It was in Bethany outside Jerusalem that Jesus raised Lazarus from the dead, an event that astonished the people. The news of it was brought to the Pharisees, who reported it to the high priest in Jerusalem. The high priest's family got together at the house of Caiaphas, where the real decision to get rid of Jesus was made. They decided

The Mount of Olives and Gethsemane

that Jesus must die before Passover, and, according to John, they sent around a messenger to say that whoever knew of his whereabouts should announce it to the authorities. A trace of the decision may be found in the Babylonian Talmud, which appeared many years later:

On the eve of the Passover, Yeshua was hanged. For forty days before the execution took place, a herald went forth and cried: he is going forth to be stoned because he had practiced sorcery and enticed Israel to apostasy. Anyone who can say anything in his favor, let him come forward and plead on his behalf. But since nothing was brought forward in his favor, he was hanged on the eve of Passover. (Sanh 43A)

From this time on, the days of Jesus were numbered. He went into hiding with his disciples at Ephraim (modern Taibeh), a village on the edge of the Judean desert (John 11:54), to prepare for his passion. It was time to fulfill his "glorification" and return to the Father. We do not know how long he stayed there, but he came back to Bethany with people who wanted to purify themselves in preparation for the feast. Each person was expected to submerge his body in the "living water" of the ritual bath before he could partake of the Passover meal.

It was six days before the temple Passover (a Saturday according to the universal calendar). Many preparations had to be made: the selection of the paschal lamb, which had to be flawless; the cleansing of the house of any yeast products; and the purchase of foods for the meal itself. People were crowding into Jerusalem. Jesus had supper at the house of Simon the leper.

The Last Supper

Although Jesus knew that the temple Passover was in six days, he said to the apostles, "You know that after two days the Passover is coming" (Matt 26: 2). He decided to celebrate Passover according to the Essene calendar, which always celebrated it on a Wednesday. He wanted to celebrate a Passover meal as his parting meal, but he had a premonition that at the time of the temple Passover he would no longer be alive. Several of the early sources (The Didascalia in Syria, Epiphanius of Salamis, Victorinus of Pettau) give the time of the Passover meal as the Tuesday evening.

We know from archaeology done at the site that the Essenes had a presence on Mount Zion. Was the Passover feast celebrated on Mount Zion in a guest house of the Essenes? According to Chapter 14 of Mark's Gospel, Jesus sent his disciples to prepare the feast. They did not know where this place was. So Jesus told them, "Go into the city, and a man carrying a jar of water will meet you" (Mark 14:13). Women usually carried the water from the well. The fact that a man was carrying the water indicates that he was unmarried. An Essene priest, perhaps? That there was someone to help suggests that Jesus already had Essene disciples in Jerusalem. (Essenes who had seen him cleanse the temple?)

Jesus arrived with the Twelve. James and other relatives may have had their own meal in another room, although apocryphal sources suggest that James was present at the Last Supper.

In following the Essene calendar and celebrating the Passover on Mount Zion, Jesus was reconciled with his family and with the Essene community.

When the meal was over, Jesus and his disciples went out across the Kidron valley to Gethsemane, where he was arrested. The guards took him to the palace of Caiaphas, the high priest who had ordered the arrest. Caiaphas sent him to his father-in-law, Annas, who had preceded him as high priest and who still asserted his power and assisted his son-in-law. For those who officiated as priests at the Temple, this Wednesday was a night like any other. Passover would be on the following Saturday. They still had two days and nights at their disposal to execute the sentence of this false messiah, if they wanted to have it over and done with before the feast began (Matt 26:4–5).

> The Madaba map (done in about 570 CE) provides an important reference to the location of Caiaphas' house. Unfortunately, the southeastern corner of the Jerusalem vignette was destroyed, but it still shows a building that is indicated as a church by two small red mosaic stones on the roof. There is no doubt that it refers to the church of St. Peter in Gallicantu.

While Caiaphas sent messengers to the various members of the Sanhedrin to convene for a court session, Annas asked Jesus a number of questions about his disciples and his teaching. Instead of an answer, Jesus said: "I have spoken openly in the world; I have always taught in synagogues and in the Temple, where all the Jews come together. I have said nothing in secret. Why do you ask me? Ask those who heard what I said to them; they know what I said" (John 18:20–21).

The Tractate Sanhedrin is a guideline for the administration of justice written down at the beginning of the second century. It referred to the lower courts as well as to the Sanhedrin. Some of the rules in this tractate would have applied to the trial against Jesus:

1. Civil suits were tried by three, capital cases by twenty-three judges (4, 1).
2. Civil suits were tried by day, and concluded by night. But capital charges must be tried by day and concluded by day. Capital charges might be concluded on the same day with a favorable verdict, but only on the morrow with an unfavorable verdict. Therefore trials were not held on the eve of the Sabbath or festivals (4, 1).
3. The Sanhedrin sat in the form of a semicircular threshing floor, so that they might see one another (4, 3).
4. If they found him not guilty, he was discharged; if not the trial was adjourned till the following day (5, 5).
5. When the trial (against a blasphemer) was finished (and the accused found guilty), the chief witness was told: "state literally what you heard," …the judge then arose and rent his garment, which rent was not to be resewn (7, 5).

Based on the Babylonian Talmud, translation under the editorship of Rabbi Dr. I. Epstein, Soncino Press.

Meanwhile Caiaphas was preparing the trial proceedings against the prisoner, to collect evidence and look for witnesses. Witnesses did come forward. "Many gave false testimony against him, and their testimony did not agree" (Mark 14:56). While waiting for the arrival of the Sanhedrin members the guards and servants of the high priest ridiculed and mocked Jesus.

Caiaphas would have informed the Sanhedrin of the charges, which were desecrating the Sabbath, the attack on the Temple, and claiming to be the Messiah. In the process of interrogation, Jesus condemned himself. When asked, "Are you the Son of God?" he did not deny it but replied, "You have said it" (Luke 22:70). And "all of them condemned him as deserving death" (Mark 14:64).

We know that two of the friends of Jesus were among the ruling body, Joseph of Arimathea and Nicodemus. They would have known the law and insisted on pondering one night on the accusation and its consequences. Jesus would have been held in custody until Thursday.

The Temple oligarchy took time to prepare and submit the indictment to the Roman procurator, Pontius Pilate. The execution of the death sentence was the responsibility of the Romans. Twenty-three members would have collected at the Temple in the chamber of Hewn Stone to officially formulate and confirm the sentence and present the bill of indictment to the Roman governor, who had just arrived from Caesarea Marittima. He stayed in the Praetorium while in Jerusalem.

> The site of the Praetorium is uncertain. It may have been in the old palace of Herod (the Citadel). This was the place later used as a quarter for the Tenth Roman Legion under Titus; or it may have been the Royal Palace of the Hasmoneans, which was just outside the Temple Mount. A large church, St. Sophia, was built here in Byzantine times; or it may have been the Antonia Fortress, north of the Temple. Since Crusader times, this has been held to be the beginning of the Via Dolorosa.

Jesus was dragged from his place of imprisonment in the dungeon of Caiaphas's house to the Praetorium. His accusers had to have a crime that was acceptable to the Roman court, for which blasphemy would not have meant much. Luke's Gospel tells us: "We have found this man perverting our nation, forbidding us to pay taxes to the emperor, and saying that he himself is the Messiah, a King" (23:2).

According to John, a strange dialogue took place between Jesus and Pilate, after which Pilate sent him to Herod Antipas, who was in town for the Passover celebration. Jesus had avoided meeting with "the fox" Herod in Galilee. And now to Herod's questions he gave no answer. He was sent back to Pilate dressed in a purple robe.

Friday morning would have been the busiest day of the whole year. It was the last day before the feast of Passover and most people were busy with preparations. We read that Pilate first attempted to have Jesus flogged with the intent of saving his life. But this did not succeed. The crowd called for his execution and threatened Pilate: "If you release this man, you are no friend

Overview of Jerusalem

of the emperor. Everyone who claims to be a king sets himself against the emperor" (John 19:12).

Jesus was condemned to death and handed over to the execution squad.

It was the fourteenth of Nisan, a Friday in the year of the Common Era, 30. In our calendar it would have been April 7.

One fact about the trial of Jesus must be made very clear: It was not the Jewish people who wanted Jesus condemned and killed. How much trouble has been caused by this false accusation, blaming Jews for the death of Jesus! The slander against the whole people led to the burning of entire communities (Crusaders), executions (Inquisition), expulsion (1492 from Spain), and pogroms. The poisoned atmosphere created by the charge of collective guilt of a people was partly responsible for giving the Nazi criminals an excuse for carrying out their neoheathen, murderous plans. This instigated the most horrible crime of modern humanity, the Holocaust, the mass murder of Jews in Auschwitz and many other places.

CHAPTER ONE

THE EVENTS AFTER THE RESURRECTION: THE YEARS 30–40

It was the eve of the feast of Passover for mainline Jews. Lambs were being slaughtered in the Temple for the evening feast. Most of the population of Jerusalem was at home preparing their houses by getting rid of all leavening, setting the table, and cooking what food was needed. For the Roman soldiers quartered in the Fortress Antonia, where they could overlook all that happened in the Temple, it was business as usual, quelling a riot or two and putting to death a few criminals.

The Romans had arrived in Palestine under General Pompey some ninety years before. Called in to solve a dispute between contenders to the Hasmonean throne, they had not left, and Palestine had been incorporated into the province of Syria. The Romans had a policy of placing friendly "client kings" on the thrones of their frontier lands to serve as buffers against unfriendly neighbors (rulers that they placed over small territories they called *tetrarchs*). Such a ruler was likely to be deposed on the slightest pretext and be replaced by another client, or by a Roman procurator.

Tiberius was emperor of Rome on April 7, 30 CE, and living on Capri. Herod Antipas was tetrarch of Galilee and in Jerusalem for the Passover feast. His brother Philip, tetrarch of Gaulinitis, Trachonitis, and Batanea, was at his home in Paneas. The Roman proconsul of Judea (the fifth to hold that position since Herod Archelaus was deposed in the year 6) was Pontius Pilate. He normally lived at Caesarea but moved to Herod's palace in the upper city of Jerusalem during times when there was likely to be trouble, such as at Passover.

Roman rule prevailed in Palestine. While the Jewish Sanhedrin had authority over religious law, they did not have the power to put someone to death. That had to be left to the Romans. And Roman justice was swift. A criminal brought before them could expect to have sentence carried out immediately. There were no public prosecutors. Charges were brought by the chief priests and members of the Sanhedrin. A prisoner was given three opportunities to defend himself. If he refused he was found guilty. On that day, Jesus was arraigned before the Roman court for claiming to be king (a challenge to Caesar). As a noncitizen, he had no rights.

The Roman orator Cicero describes crucifixion as the most cruel and frightful way to die. The method was devised to wring the most supreme torment and suffering. Introduced three hundred years earlier, picked up from the Persians, it was inflicted for murder, banditry, piracy, and rebellion. The victim was first scourged and made to carry the cross-beam to the place of execution. All shred of dignity or humanity was taken away. He was stripped naked and nailed in position. Death usually came by suffocation and it could take days. Sometimes the process was hastened by the soldiers breaking the leg bones of the victim.

Jesus was condemned to death on that Friday and the sentence carried out with haste. For three hours he writhed in torment while the execution squad threw dice for the seamless linen garment he had been wearing when arrested (John 19:23–24). According to Mark's Gospel (15:34), he cried out in agony, "My God, my God, why have you forsaken me?"

Countryside near Nazareth

The women who had followed Jesus from Galilee stood horrified and helpless near the wall close by, together with his mother and John, the Beloved Disciple. John's Gospel records that as he hung on the cross, "When Jesus saw his mother, and the disciple whom he loved standing beside her, he said to his mother, 'Woman, here is your son.' Then he said to the disciple, 'Here is your mother.' And from that hour the disciple took her into his own home" (John 19:26–27).

The two families, the one of Nazareth and the one chosen by him at Capernaum, who had been virtually separated during his public ministry, now came together as he hung on the cross. Over his head hung the signboard (titalus) on which was written "Jesus, the Nazorean, King of the Jews." This was the crime for which he was being put to death. Mark tells us that officials from the high priest were present.

The crowd passing by on their way to their Passover feast mocked and taunted him. Psalm 22 comes to mind:

> All who see me mock at me;
> they make mouths at me, they shake their heads;
> "Commit your cause to the LORD; let him deliver—
> let him rescue the one in whom he delights!"

When the Roman soldiers determined that he was dead by thrusting a lance through his side, Joseph of Arimathea and Nicodemus, both members of the Sanhedrin and friends of Jesus, climbed a ladder to free his body from the nails, and then placed him in the arms of his mother. What excruciating sadness, hopelessness, and despair encompassed the little group! The scene of the mother holding the lifeless body of her only son would inspire artists for generations to come.

It was growing dark. Nicodemus had brought with him a hundred pounds of myrrh and aloes to anoint the body, but there was no time for that. The soldiers scurried about nervously, ordering the place vacated. The body was wrapped in a linen shroud and carried by the men to a new tomb nearby, which Joseph had bought for himself. The wailing women held closely to his mother looking on the body of her child for the last time. A large stone was moved in front and he was hidden from view. Then they walked slowly down the hill and back through the gate into the city where Passover celebrations had just begun. Jesus, their beloved, their hope, was dead. It was finished.

The Beginning

All of his male friends, with the exception of John, had deserted when Jesus was arrested, hiding from the authorities who might start questioning them. It was not unusual to round up the followers and mete out the same punishment to them. They must have spent the next day dazed and devastated. They had been with him for three years, seen him perform wondrous works, and heard his words spoken with authority and confidence. He was so full of kindness and compassion and had attracted such crowds of people. They had thought he was the expected Messiah. Some had even anticipated a special place when he came into his kingdom. They had left everything to follow him. Now it had come to nothing. Crucifixion meant the clear refutation of any claim to be the Messiah. One who "hung on a tree" was accursed by God (Deut 21:22). This form of death had stamped out the messianic hope once and for all.

The women of the company, more practical than the men, bought spices and oils and mixed them. These women had been with Jesus all the way from Galilee, supporting him and his ministry. They had not deserted him, but stood at the foot of his cross to give what solace they could. It was the custom in Jewish burials to anoint the body before interment, but Jesus had been buried so hurriedly on Friday that there was no time for this service. They would see to it that the last burial rites were performed.

Already rumors began to circulate that the earth had shaken and the curtain of the Temple had been rent in two at the exact moment he died. Some reported that they had seen the bodies of people who had died come out of their tombs, while others said that even the executioner had professed that this was no ordinary man. But the day must have been one of hopeless misery for his followers.

The Resurrection

On Sunday at dawn, Mary Magdalene and the other women came to the tomb bearing their last gift. But in the first light of the dawn, they saw that the stone had been rolled away and the tomb was empty! Jesus was not there! Had someone been there before them and taken him away? There had been all those rumors of strange things happening. Maybe his body was somewhere on the ground. In the lighting dawn they looked around them. Then they heard a voice ringing in their ears, "Why do you look for the living among the dead? He is not here, but has risen" (Luke 24:4–7).

The amazed women fled back through the city gate, across to the Essene quarter to the guest house where they knew the others were hiding. It was early. The men were still sleeping. Mary Magdalene shouted the news: "He is risen! The tomb is empty!"

The most extraordinary thing in the history of the world had happened. The women were proclaiming it.

John got to his feet and started running toward Golgotha. Peter pulled on his cloak and quickly followed. "Then Simon Peter came, following him, and went into the tomb. He saw the linen wrappings lying there, and the cloth that had been on Jesus' head, not lying with the linen wrappings, but rolled up in a place by itself. Then the other disciple, who reached the tomb first, also went in, and he saw and believed" (John 20:6–8).

The Essenes and the Pharisees believed in resurrection. The question had come up when Jesus had argued with the Sadducees, who were not believers. In Jewish thought,

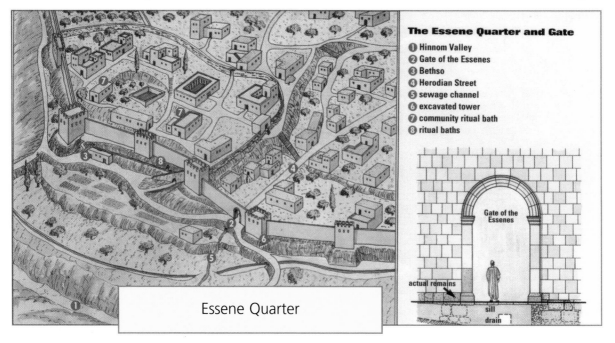

The Essene Quarter and Gate
1. Hinnom Valley
2. Gate of the Essenes
3. Bethso
4. Herodian Street
5. sewage channel
6. excavated tower
7. community ritual bath
8. ritual baths

Gate of the Essenes

actual remains

sill
drain

Essene Quarter

two men had been taken up to heaven, Enoch and Elijah, who would return in the end days. But one rising from the dead here and now, that was not heard of.

Did Peter rub his eyes wondering what these women were saying? He must have thought Mary Magdalene hysterical. So overcome with grief, she was imagining things.

"He is risen! The tomb is empty!…He is risen! The tomb is empty!…He is risen! The tomb is empty!"

Mary Magdalene's voice was wondrous. The cry echoed through the halls waking the sleepers.

How bewildered the two apostles were! Jesus had been crucified. He had died. He had been buried. No man could rise from the dead! They knew their scriptures. And the scriptures touched upon resurrection only vaguely. It was after the Maccabean War that the idea that the just and pious would rise and be rewarded had come up. That would happen at the end of days. The Book of Enoch speaks of resurrection:

> In those days the earth will give back what was entrusted to it.
> Sheol will return what it has received
> And hell will give back what it owes.
> For in those days the Elected One will arise
> And choose the good and holy from those who died.

Surely as the group clung together that day a new reality penetrated their consciousness. Jesus had risen from the dead and entered into a new sphere of being! All their hopes were justified. The crucifixion had not been an end but a beginning of something far greater.

The news spread quickly. Their mourning changed to joyful expectation.

WRITTEN ACCOUNTS OF THE APPEARANCES OF JESUS

The oldest written report of the resurrection is given in 1 Corinthians 15, which was written between 52 and 57. 1 Corinthians is one of the authentic letters written by Saint Paul:

> For I handed on to you as of first importance what I in turn received; that Christ died for our sins in accordance with the scriptures, and that he was buried, that he was raised on the third day in accordance with the scriptures, and that he appeared to Cephas, then to the twelve. Then he appeared to more than five hundred brothers and sisters at one time, most of whom are still alive, though some have died. Then he appeared to James, to all the apostles.

John's Gospel, which was written much later, tells of his appearing first to Mary Magdalene, who had gone back to the tomb sobbing. There she saw a figure who she thought was the gardener: "Sir, if you have carried him away, tell me where you have laid him and I will take him away" (John 20:15). And the figure answered in a voice she knew well: "Mary!"

Luke records that two disciples were on their way to Emmaus that same day when Jesus appeared to them, and later that same evening he appeared to ten of the apostles also. Thomas was missing at that time, but later encountered him. Luke also relates in Acts 13:30 that Jesus was seen by witnesses who had come from Galilee, but it does not specify who they were or when he appeared.

According to John, Jesus appeared to seven as they were fishing in Galilee (John 21:4–6). He cooked a meal of fish for them after they had made a great haul (153 fish) at his command. So overwhelmed were they that they did not even ask who he was for "they knew it was the Lord."

How and when Jesus appeared to James is a question. First Corinthians relates that James was the last to see him. In the apocryphal Gospel to the Hebrews, which some scholars think is an Aramaic version of Matthew's Gospel (not to be confused with the canonical Letter to the Hebrews), it is reported that James had taken an oath that he would not eat any bread from the moment he drank the Lord's cup until he would see him rise from sleeping. Perhaps James expected the resurrection. This apocryphal gospel was held in high regard by such Church Fathers as Origen and Jerome. The latter cites the text:

> And when the Lord had given the linen cloth to the servant of the priest, he went to James and appeared to him. For James had sworn that he would not eat bread from that hour in which he had drunk the cup of the Lord until he should see him raised from among them that sleep. And shortly thereafter the Lord said: "Bring a table and bread!" And immediately it is added, he took the bread, blessed it and brake it and gave it to James the Just and said to him: "My brother, eat your bread, for the Son of Man is risen from among them that sleep." (Jerome, *De Viris Illustribus* 2)

He Is Risen!

The resurrection of Jesus from the dead changed everything for his followers. The words *He is risen* are the foundation of Christianity. These words contain Christology in a nutshell. From *He is risen* would spring *Son of God, the Pre-Existent Messiah, the Incarnate Wisdom.*

After the Ascension

The apparitions of Jesus seem to have continued for about forty days. During this time, John relates that the fishermen had gone back to Galilee. Matthew places the last appearance of Jesus on a hill in Galilee where he commissioned them:

All authority in heaven and earth has been given to me. Go therefore and make disciples of all nations, baptizing them in the name of the Father and of the Son and of the Holy Spirit, and teaching them to obey everything I have commanded you. And remember I am with you always, to the very end of the age. (Matt 28:18–20)

Luke's gospel places the last appearance of Jesus on the Mount of Olives in Jerusalem, perhaps for his own theological purposes.

Whichever the case, we know from the archaeology done at these places that the followers of Jesus soon settled in Capernaum and Nazareth in the north. But many who had come with him from Galilee remained in Jerusalem.

There are several ancient traditions about where this early group of followers lived in Jerusalem. One tradi-

The ancient synagogue at Capernaum

tion claims that there was a house of John the Evangelist on what is today known as Mount Zion. The German scholar Wilhelm Wuellner has surmised that John's fishing business required his frequent presence in Jerusalem and that he owned a house there. Another early tradition claims that John was himself a priest. There were twenty-four divisions of the priesthood scattered all over the land. Most only went to Jerusalem when it was their turn to serve, which would account for the high priest having known John, as it says in John 18:15. And early Church Father, Epiphanius (315–403), later bishop of Salamis in Cyprus, mentions a tradition that James, the brother of Jesus, and the sons of Zebedee, John and James, kept one and the same household and that Mary lived with them.

But in the early weeks we find them still guests in the upper room. Archaeological excavations done by Jacob Pinkerfield, Bargil Pixner, and others in the southwest corner of Jerusalem strongly suggest that the "upper room" where they were gathered together to pray was close to the confines of the Essene community.

MOUNT ZION

The supposed location of Mount Zion changed several times during Israel's long history. The original Mount Zion was a Jebusite fortress conquered by David around the year 1000 BCE (2 Sam 5:7, 9). It stood on an elevated rock over the Gihon fountain. There David had erected a tent, to which he brought the Ark of the Covenant in solemn procession from Baala Jehudah (1 Sam 6:2) as a unifying symbol of the twelve tribes. His son Solomon built a temple on a hill to the north of it.

Zion II, where the Temple stood, was the abode of God where God lived in the midst of his people (Isa 60:14; Amos 6:7). The second Temple was destroyed in 70 CE, but the idea of Zion outlasted the destruction of its established symbol. At the turn of the first century, the southwestern hill of Jerusalem assumed the name Zion (Zion III).

The early Christian community saw in that hill the cradle of their messianic movement, the place of Christian origins. They probably reasoned (as did Flavius Josephus) that this hill was the original Zion, where the fortress of David stood (archaeologically wrong). They dared to transfer the name to this hill.

Epiphanius was a native Palestinian. In his writings he tells about the journey of the emperor Hadrian (130 CE) to see Jerusalem, and speaks of "the mother of all the churches," the first Christian church, as still standing. He called it a church even though there were no church buildings before the fourth century. It was in fact a Jewish-Christian synagogue, as we shall see later.

Pentecost

The feast of Pentecost *(Shavuot)* was approaching. The group prepared for it by gathering together to pray:

> They went to the room upstairs where they were staying, Peter, and John, and James, and Andrew, Philip and Thomas, Bartholomew and Matthew, James son of Alphaeus, and Simon the Zealot, and Judas son of James. All these were constantly devoting themselves to prayer, together with certain women, including Mary the mother of Jesus, as well as his brothers. (Acts 1:13–14)

Pentecost was one of the great pilgrim feasts, when all Jews were called to Jerusalem. Indeed, the Acts of the Apostles tells us that there were Jews from Mesopotamia, Cappadocia, Pontus, Asia, Phrygia, Pamphylia, Egypt , Libya, Rome, and Crete, as well as Parthians, Medes, and Elamites. The firstfruits of the harvest were brought to the Temple. Bread made from the new wheat was eaten. Wine from last year's grapes was drunk. The receiving of the law at Sinai was commemorated and the covenant was renewed.

But it was a movable feast. It occurred fifty days after Passover counting from the day after the Shabbat of Passover. In counting, however, Pharisees, Sadducees, and Essenes differed.

The Pharisees used the *Omer* counting from Leviticus 23:15. They regarded the Passover itself as a Shabbat and they counted fifty days from the day after Passover. The Sadducees, on the contrary, counted from the Saturday after Passover. The Essenes counted fifty days after the whole week of unleavened bread. They celebrated eight days of Passover and then counted from the Sabbath that came after the eight days. Their Pentecost was therefore the last to be observed.

We know from the Dead Sea Scrolls that the whole Essene community was required to come together in a general assembly once a year to renew the covenant. This may have been their day. Acts 2:5 tells us that staying together in Jerusalem were devout men, *Eulabeis*. There was no official name for the Essenes. They were known variously as Eulabeis (the Devout People) or the Hebrew equivalent Hasideans (the Pious Ones). Apparently the group of Jesus' followers celebrated according to the Essene calendar.

"Hasideans" are mentioned in Maccabees 1 as those observant people who had gone to the desert where they could live a total Jewish life, which was impossible under the Greeks in Jerusalem.

The term *Eulabeis* is used in other places in Luke's work: Simeon in the temple (Luke 2:25), Ananias of Damascus (Acts 22:12), and those who buried Stephen (Acts 8:2), as well as those who were gathered for Pentecost.

The general opinion of scholars is that *Hessaioi, Essenoi,* and *Eulabeis* could refer to the whole Hasidic movement, who were the Essenes.

Philo of Alexandria refers to Alexandrian *Therapeutes,* meaning "very observant." It was a religious movement in Egypt that was probably related to the Essenes. Some speculate that Philo was himself a Therapeute.

What happened that Pentecost morning to change the small group of followers from a frightened, bewildered people into emboldened, powerful, self-assured speakers, so enthusiastic that they were accused of having drunk too much "new" wine? They had prayed together for nine days, and on the morning of Pentecost *(Shavuot),* "suddenly from the heavens, there came a noise like a violent wind, and it filled the entire house where they were sitting. Divided tongues, as of fire, appeared among them, and a tongue rested on each of them. All were filled with the Holy Spirit" (Acts 2:2–4).

Was it the recognition that they were no longer alone? The Spirit of Jesus permeated them, and they knew with certainty that far from being the end of their hopes and longings this was the beginning! One can imagine the joy on their faces as they went about telling the good news with such assurance. "They made bold proclamations as the Spirit prompted them," the book of Acts conveys. "Amazed," "astonished" crowds, already crammed into Jerusalem for the feast, circled around them to listen:

Jesus of Nazareth, a man attested to you by God with deeds of power, wonders, and signs that God did through him among you, as you yourselves know…this man, handed over to you according to the definite plan and foreknowledge of God, you crucified and killed by the hands of those outside the law. But God raised him up having freed him from death because it was impossible for him to be held in its power. (Acts 2:22–24)

Their passion caught fire. Many were baptized by Peter and the others. Acts tells us three thousand were added in one day. The message that would change the world was being delivered. Pentecost was the day of the launching of Christianity.

The Community Develops Under Essene Influence

It indeed appears that there was a connection between the Essenes of Jerusalem and the followers of Jesus. We learn from Acts that a whole group of priests joined their number (Acts 6:7). These priests could not have been Sadducees since they were opposed to the new sect. Nor could they have been Pharisees since they were generally not priests. They must have come from the Essenes. Let us examine several instances of Essene influence in the beginning church of Jerusalem.

Peter and the Eleven had to choose a replacement for Judas (Acts 1:26), which they did before the feast of Pentecost. They cast lots, the lot fell on Matthias, and Matthias was enrolled with the eleven apostles (Acts 1:23–26). Election by lot was a typical Essene way of selection (1QS 6:8–23). The whole Essene community participated in choosing leaders after a thorough examination of the candidates. Possibly Matthias came from the Essenes. According to tradition he was a very abstemious man (as of course were the Essenes). In the Copper Scroll of the Essenes a "house of Matthias" is mentioned.

Also striking is the rite of initiation into the two groups. In normative Judaism, circumcision was the rite of admission into the covenant. The Essenes, instead of requiring circumcision for admission, baptized. (This is discussed extensively by Nodet and Taylor in *The Origins of Christianity*.) Ritual baptism

Mikvah, or Essene ritual bath

with water was the conclusion of a process of initiation. The ritual for baptizing of the new initiate is described in their writings:

> Whoever is acceptable into the community shall be cleansed from all his sins by the Holy Spirit uniting him to the truth, and his inquiry shall be expiated by the spirit of righteousness and humility. And when his flesh is sprinkled with purifying water and sanctified with cleansing water it shall be made clean by the humble submission of his soul to all the precepts of God. (1Q 8–10)

Similarly, the rite of baptism admitted the candidate to the Sacred Meal among both the Essenes and Christians.

The Essenes partook of a community meal (principally of bread and wine), which distinguished them from other Jewish groups. Among the followers of Jesus, once baptism had been administered, the candidate was admitted to participation in the Eucharist.

The community of goods, the social system of the Essenes by which everything was shared in common, was adopted by a group of the early Christians (Acts 2:44).

The Holy Spirit was common to both groups. The term *Holy Spirit* appears frequently in the Essene literature, as it does in the Acts of the Apostles.

The hierarchy established by the Jerusalem church suggests Essene influence. Twelve elders were chosen to govern.

The Essenes were involved in healing ministry, as were the early Christians. A cripple was cured by the Beautiful Gate of the Temple. (We know from the Temple scroll that he would not have been permitted to enter the Temple in his condition.)

Times of prayer—morning, noon, and evening for the Christian community—coincide with Essene times of prayer. Other groups only prayed twice a day.

Pentecost became the main feast for the early church, as it was for the Essenes.

Based on all of this evidence it appears certain that the early group on Mount Zion was in close association with the Essene community and influenced by them.

The Family of Jesus

Many of the Nazoreans (of the clan of Jesus) moved to Jerusalem, some perhaps even before his death. The apparition to the five hundred may have included them (1 Cor 15:6). While none of them had been active in his ministry, they were now believers. These men were builders by trade and needed work. Much building was going on in Jerusalem, where the Temple was still under construction, and the surrounding villages.

Simon, son of Cleophas (brother of Joseph of Nazareth), could have been some twenty years old at that time and may have come with his father to Jerusalem. Some authors believe that he was the companion mentioned with Cleophas, when Jesus joined them on the way to Emmaus (Luke 24:13–35). This village had been destroyed by the cruel Quintilius Varus in 6 CE as a result of a small uprising, and perhaps was being rebuilt at this time. Simon and Cleophas may have worked there.

Leadership

The message of Jesus spread rapidly after Pentecost: "Therefore let the entire house of Israel know with certainty that God has made him both Lord and Messiah, this Jesus whom you crucified" (Acts 2:36).

Great numbers of followers were added daily in Jerusalem. The "devout men" who had been in the city for Pentecost would have carried the message back to their hometowns in Asia Minor, Cappadocia, Mesopotamia, Cyrene, Egypt, Libya, and other places.

Peter and John, who had been with him from the beginning, saw evangelization as their main task (Acts 6:2). Tirelessly, they went about preaching the word and curing the sick. (One scholar suggests that it was their curing of the sick without payment that drew people to the early church.) The Acts of the Apostles tells us that people were drawn to them because of their power (Acts 3:13), and that many sick were brought to them (Acts 5:12).

Such behavior did not go unnoticed. News spread quickly in this city of eighty thousand inhabitants. These bold men were drawing attention, spreading new ideas, disturbing the status quo. They were claiming that Jesus was the expected Messiah. This could not be allowed. The irritated authorities had them arrested and imprisoned.

But they were not without friends in high places. Gamaliel intervened at the trial of Peter (Acts 5:33–39) and questioned the movement's survival. He gave the defenders the benefit of the doubt. Nicodemus and Joseph of Arimathea were members of the Sanhedrin. They understood what was happening. They were sympathizers. Was Nicodemus a sympathizer of the Essenes? John's Gospel recounts an encounter between Jesus and Nicodemus: "Very truly I tell you, no one can enter the kingdom of God without being born of water and Spirit" (John 3:5). The rite of water and the spirit would have been familiar to Essene ears.

Two Groups

As the days and weeks passed and the number of converts grew, organization was necessary. Two assemblages emerged within the growing community, the Greek- and the

Aramaic-speaking groups. Each group prayed in its own language and attended different synagogues.

The Aramaic-speaking group followed the social system of the Essenes, "the community of goods," and may have done so on a voluntary basis. The story of Ananias and Sapphira (Acts 5:4) indicates that there was a preparatory stage if they wanted to contribute their property to the common treasury. Once they were received into the community it became obligatory.

Tomb of Jesus

It seems that the Greek-speaking Jews did not usually participate in the community of goods, although Barnabas sold his field in Cyprus and gave money to the apostles. Barnabas, an idealistic man, may have been the link between the two groups. The Greeks may have been the wealthier element. Mary, the mother of John Mark and sister of Barnabas, was Greek-speaking. We know that a group met in her home to pray (Acts 12:12). She had a prominent house in Jerusalem that had a courtyard with a gate for security. She also had a maid, Rhoda, indicating that she may have been prosperous.

But the two factions were not without strife. Greek-speaking disciples complained about the distribution of alms to the Greek widows, who they did not think were being fairly treated. The apostles seem to have been busy spreading the news but were not doing follow-up. Eventually the issue was solved by ordaining seven men to take care of these problems. We hear for the first time of deacons. Their names, Stephen, Philip, Prochorus, Niconor, Timon, Parmenas, and Nicholaus suggest that they were Hellenist, that is, Jews who had been born in a foreign land and whose native tongue was Greek. Their purpose was to serve at table, but they eventually became evangelists unable to withhold their enthusiasm for spreading the good news.

Stephen, the First Martyr

Had Stephen lived, would he have outdone Paul in oratory? The suggestion that Stephen was a pupil of Gamaliel, as was Paul, cannot be verified. He belonged to the synagogues of the "Libertines," made up of Jews from Cyrene, Alexandria, Cilicia, and Asia, and he was publicly acknowledged as a man "of good standing, full of the Spirit and of wisdom," "a man full of faith, and the Holy Spirit," "full of grace and power" (Acts 6:3–8). But members of his synagogue accused him of blasphemy, a charge that called for the death penalty. Stephen gave a brilliant defense of himself before the Sanhedrin, while "all who sat in the council looked intensely at him and they saw that his face was like the face of an angel."

Stephen's accusers took him out of the city to stone him to death. The law required that the company lay their hands on his head before stoning. Perhaps it was at this time that "he knelt down and cried out in a loud voice: 'Lord, do not hold this sin against them'" (Acts 7:59). The witnesses threw down their garments at the feet of Saul (we most commonly know him by his Roman name, Paul) that they might be more ready for the task of stoning.

The community had been harassed all along, but Stephen became the first to shed his blood for the new movement. "Devout men" (Essenes?) carried away his body for burial.

One can imagine the dread that descended on his friends. According to Eusebius, a panic situation prevailed, and many of the Greek-speakers left Jerusalem. They did not give up their belief, however. Wherever they went, they saw it as an opportunity for missionary activity, proclaiming the faith first to Jews in Samaria and then to Jews farther afield.

Paul

Watching someone die, especially so brutally and with such courage, could not be overlooked or taken lightly. The last words uttered by the dying Stephen must have left a great impression on the mind of Paul.

Was Stephen's death the turning point for the church? Jerome Murphy O'Connor suggests that if Paul had been in Jerusalem before the year 30, he would certainly have heard of Jesus and of his crucifixion. As a Pharisee he would have believed in the resurrection. Indeed if Jesus had risen from the dead, then for Paul, he was all that his followers claimed him to be, the long-awaited Messiah of the Jews. It was one thing to claim that Jesus had risen. It was another to give one's life for the belief. Was it as he watched Stephen die that Paul began to vacillate? The decisive hour of his conversion was on the way to Damascus, as the Acts of the Apostles relates. Saul fell on the ground and heard a voice saying to him, "'Saul, Saul, why do you persecute me?' He asked 'Who are you, Lord?' The reply came 'I am Jesus whom you are persecuting. But get up and enter the city and you will be told what you are to do'" (Acts: 9:4–7).

Once in Damascus, he was baptized there by "a pious one," Ananias, and soon afterward he started to proclaim in the synagogue that Jesus was the Son of God.

Leadership in Jerusalem

Peter and John were still active in the church in Jerusalem for its first decade, but mindful of the admonition of Jesus, "Go teach all nations," they planned to leave. James, the brother of Jesus, was leader of the Aramaic-speaking group and assumed a stronger role. Because of his extraordinary piety and his Jewish loyalty he was able to keep the people around him safe, forming a protecting wall around them. He was known as James the Righteous (the *Tzadik*). Hegesippus says that he wore out his knees praying in the temple. And he was Jewish to the core. As the apostles scattered to other places, James remained in Jerusalem and became Jerusalem's first bishop.

Eusebius tells us: "Peter and James and John, after the Ascension of the Savior, did not claim preeminence because the Savior had specially honored them, but chose James the Righteous (the *Tzadik*) as bishop of Jerusalem."

W. Nauch, who examined the early ministerial jobs in the church, claims that in the Essene community there was a supervisor *(megaqqer)*, which is very similar to the overseer. Joachim Jeremias believes that there is a relationship between the *megaqqer* and the bishop, a shepherd (see Acts 20:28).

There may have been a deeper reason for the main apostles to renounce assuming the post of bishop of the Jerusalem community. James was the fittest man for the job. Besides being the brother of Jesus and a scion of the Davidic family, he may also have had connections with the Essene community. He had celebrated the Jewish feasts according to the Essene calendar (John 7:2–6) and may well have done this in the Essene guest house. The large group of priests that embraced the faith may have been acquaintances of James.

James played a leading role because he was the oldest brother of Jesus. At the Council of Jerusalem (Acts 15:15), he referred to the prophesy of Amos (9:11–12):

> On that day I will raise up the booth of David that is fallen, and repair its breaches, and raise up its ruins, and rebuild it as in the day of old, in order that they may possess the remnant of Edom and all the nations who are called by my name.

Amos's quotation was particularly important to the Essenes. From their commentaries we have the following:

> This is the branch of David who will arise with the interpreter of the Law and who will reside on Zion at the end of the days; as it is written I will

raise up the tabernacle of David which is fallen. This tabernacle, which is fallen, will arise to redeem Israel. (4Q, Flor. 1, 10–13)

The Essene believers must have been staunch supporters of the Davidic descent of Jesus and James, his brother. They may not have so staunchly supported the conversion of gentiles.

The First Gentiles Join the Church

The conversion of the gentiles happened on home territory when Peter went to Jaffa and Lod. While he was in Jaffa he received a message to bring the good news to the gentile family of Cornelius in Caesarea Maritima. Acts records that at the same time, he was inspired in a vision that the dietary laws of the Jews were no longer valid. Peter went to the house of Cornelius where he was met by relatives and close friends of his host and he began to preach to them about Jesus. The whole household was converted: "Now the apostles and the believers who were in Judea heard that the Gentiles had also accepted the word of God" (Acts 11:1).

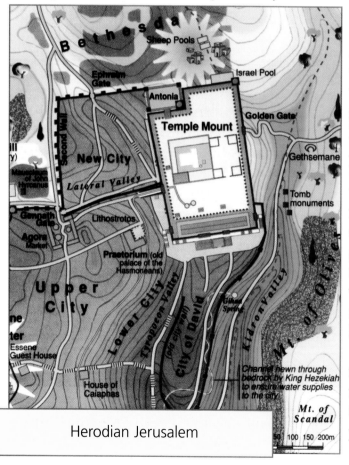

Herodian Jerusalem

Upon Peter's return to Jerusalem, the Jewish community was shocked to hear that he was mixing with gentiles (Acts 10), and that the word was now also preached to the gentiles and that they had accepted it. Jerusalem had sent evangelizers to Antioch and Samaria to convert Jews, but now Peter had taken the initiative to spread it to the gentiles. On his return to Jerusalem Peter met strong criticism, not against preaching to the gentiles or baptizing them but against table community with them. To eat with them was frowned upon. Many thought that gentile converts would have to become Jewish proselytes.

Behind it all was a conviction that proselyte believers were bound to the dietary and purity laws of the Old Testament. Either the converted pagans must obey the law as Jewish

Christians did or must live separately. The community in Jerusalem insisted on their Jewish rites. There was a doubt about the sincerity of the converted.

Although in his last command in Galilee Jesus had instructed his disciples to preach the gospel to the whole world, he had never said anything about the obligations the gentiles would have to take upon themselves. The big questions were about the dietary laws and circumcision.

When the gentiles heard the good news they readily accepted it, but how well? Was there a division? It is doubtful whether a peaceful attitude between the Jewish Christians and the representatives of the gentile Christians really existed. A decade later the difficulties were brought into sharp contrast at the Council of Jerusalem. There must have been many discussions in between, especially when the news of Paul's and Barnabas's activities came back to Jerusalem.

Prayer and Worship in the Early Community

It is unclear at what point the community developed their own liturgy and way of worship. Where did they baptize? They must have asked for pure, life-giving water, because they expected to be reborn to a new purity. One scholar has suggested that the first community may have been allowed to use the ritual baths of the Essenes on Mount Zion. The Spring of Siloam would also have provided such living water.

The followers of Jesus "devoted themselves to the apostles' teaching and fellowship, to the breaking of bread and the prayers" (Acts 2:42). The Eucharist was celebrated in the homes on Sundays; it is not known who presided. Were any of the presiders women? The community continued to meet in synagogues. The Roman law allowed the Jews to profess their faith publicly in synagogues, and as long as the community met thus they were protected by law. But they also worshipped in places associated with the events in the life of Jesus, such as Bethlehem, the Holy Sepulcher, and the "elone," the grotto in the garden of olives where the apostles were waiting and sleeping during Jesus' agony in the garden. (The Church of the Our Father stands there now.) They went up to the temple at the hour of prayer (Acts 3:1), which was three o'clock in the afternoon (the ninth hour). Peter himself prayed in Joppa at noon, the "sixth hour" (Acts 10:9), and the Jerusalem community also met for night prayer (Acts 12:5–12). This was unusual. The Essenes prayed also at night but no other Jewish community had the tradition of night prayer.

They expressed their joy in songs and hymns. Luke used the hymns of the first community and put them into the mouths of Zechariah, Mary, Simeon, and the angels. Perhaps first thing in the morning they recited what Luke later recorded: "By the tender compassion of our God, the dawn from on high will break upon us, to give light to those in darkness and the shadow of death, to guide our feet into the way of peace" (Luke 1:78).

Women in the Early Community

Two women are named in association with activity in Jerusalem during this time: Mary, the mother of John Mark, and Rhoda, her servant (Acts 12:12, 13). Nevertheless, since half the population was female, it is to be expected that many women were engaged in service in this community. There were widows, both in the Aramaic- and Greek-speaking circles. Mary, the wife of Cleophas (mother of Simon), stood by the mother of Jesus at the cross. Since her husband lived in Jerusalem (Luke 24:18), she doubtless lived there too. Mary and Martha, the sisters of Lazarus, resided not far away. It is possible that the women who had followed Jesus to Jerusalem, Joanna, Susanna (Luke 8:2–4), and others, remained there. In the Greek Orthodox church of Mary Magdalene on the Mount of Olives, there is an icon of Mary Magdalene confronting Emperor Tiberius to complain about the behavior of Pontius Pilate. While this is, of course, apocryphal, it indicates the importance in which Mary Magdalene was held in the early church.

There were numerous converts to the new sect. Since baptism was done by immersion, did women baptize women? Acts tells that seven deacons were appointed by the laying on of hands. We know that Paul had at least one woman deacon, Phoebe, and that women taught and prophesized. The liberating message of Christ to women was taken seriously, and women served with men in the establishment of the church worldwide. This is testified to in the Acts of the Apostles and the letters of Paul. We can presume such to have been the case in Jerusalem.

The Influence of Politics

Political events had their impact on the community. Eusebius recalls that Pilate was involved in such calamities that he was forced to become his own executioner and to punish himself with his own hand. Divine justice, it seems, was not slow to overtake him. The facts are recorded by those Greeks who have chronicled the Olympiads together with the events occurring in each.

All governors of provinces reported to Rome the local situation, so that Rome might be aware of all that was going on. Eusebius claims that Pilate sent a report of the resurrection to Tiberius, but there is no way to verify this.

One of the judges of Jesus, Herod Antipas, was having his problems in Galilee. His brother Philip, the tetrarch of Gaulinitis, Trachonitis, and Batanea, died in 34. He had beautified the capital of his region, Caesarea Philippi, which was named after him to distinguish it from Caesarea Maritima. He raised the village of Bethsaida to a polis (a city) and renamed it Julius, after the mother of Emperor Tiberius. Philip loved Bethsaida and wanted his grave to be made there. He started building some outstanding edifices in Bethsaida, but since he died so soon his work did not get very far. Five of the apostles had come from this town—Peter, Andrew, James, John, and Philip—and Jesus conducted much of the ministry in and around Bethsaida.

In his later years, the tetrarch Philip married Salome, the daughter of Herodias, who had danced before Antipas and demanded the head of John the Baptist. Philip had remained childless, and after his death Antipas apparently had a claim to the land of his brother. But so did Aretas the Nabatean king (the former father-in-law of Antipas), who intended to seize that territory for himself since Herod Antipas had repudiated his daughter for Herodias. It came to war between the two armies in the region of Gaulanitis. The troops of Antipas were badly defeated because Philip's troops, who were supposed to join him, deserted. They had loved John the Baptist, and Josephus states that they deserted in revenge for John's execution.

In the end, the emperor gave Philip's tetrarchy to the grandson of Herod the Great, Agrippa I. Antipas was exiled to the Pyrenees, where he died. Agrippa would eventually become king over all the land and rule the territories his grandfather had ruled.

Gaius Caligula became emperor in 37. He hated the Jewish race and had his own statue placed in synagogues in the Diaspora. In Jerusalem he attempted to have the Temple made into his own temple and called "the temple of the Younger Gaius." This caused revolts in Jerusalem and must have outraged the nascent community on Mount Zion.

We have no way of knowing how many joined the community of believers in Jerusalem in its first ten years. Acts tells that eight deacons had to be added early on to take care of the Greek speakers alone and alludes to many others who were baptized (three thousand in one day!). Doubtless many converts were made among those who were not permanent residents but were on pilgrimage to the holy city.

CHAPTER TWO

COMMUNITY LIFE, TENSIONS,
THE COUNCIL OF JERUSALEM
THE YEARS 40–50

The Roman Empire stretched like a colossus from Britain to Syria, encompassing all of modern North Africa, Europe, and Turkey to the Euphrates. The genius of Rome lay in its governing. Its territory was divided into provinces and its ablest men sent to rule. Its mixed population is estimated to have been fifty-four million, the vast majority of whom were noncitizens with no civil rights. Great cities were built or renovated: Ephesus, Alexandria, Antioch, and Philippi. The cities of Jeresh, Baalbeck, and Bilbos were less than one hundred miles from Jerusalem. These cities displayed power and permanence and testified that Rome would live forever. Roman religion was displayed in magnificent temples built to the Capitoline gods. Theaters, gymnasia, public baths, triumphal arches, wide boulevards, forums, libraries, and houses of prostitution serviced the patrician class. Roman cruelty to "lesser" humans was put on view in their coliseums and circuses. Roads, with staging posts and inns, stretched across the Empire, making travel relatively easy. And Roman ships carrying goods and passengers sailed through the Mediterranean, which the Romans called Mare Nostrum (our sea). Latin was the language spoken in the west of the Empire; Greek was spoken in the east. In Syria and Palestine, people spoke Aramaic.

Freedom of religion was permitted provided it did not interfere with Roman ideology. The cult of the emperor flourished as governors who wished to curry favor

Theater at Sepphoris, an important Greco-Roman town near Nazareth

dedicated a new place of worship to the current ruler and priests offered sacrifice to his honor.

On the death of Tiberius in 37, Gaius became emperor of Rome. His nickname, Caligula or "little boots," had been given him by soldiers when he went as a child on campaign with his father Germanicus. Charming child he may have been, but Caligula was a cruel and despotic ruler. Eusebius tells us:

> So incalculable was his behavior towards everyone, especially the Jewish race. He hated them so bitterly that in city after city he seized the synagogues and filled them with images of himself...And in the holy city he tried to change the sanctuary and transform it into a temple of his own, to be called the temple of Jupiter the Glorious, the Younger Gaius.

Philo throws some light on this incident. It appears that in the year 40, the Jews in Jamnia destroyed an altar erected by the pagan Greeks. When news of it reached Caligula, he ordered his statue set up in the Temple. Philo records that thousands of Jews were prepared to be killed rather than see this "abomination of desolation." The legate of Syria, Publius Petronius, managed to postpone carrying out the order.

Caligula and Agrippa Herod had grown up together in Rome and were great friends, despite the emperor's general dislike of the Jews. It was the custom to send sons of satellite kings to be educated in Rome, where they were indoctrinated with Roman ideology. All of the boys in the Herod family had been so educated. Agrippa was the grandson of the great Herod and heir apparent, since his reigning uncles had no sons.

This arrogant young man was a spendthrift, way over his head in debt, and despite his linkage to the royal family, was sent to debtors' prison in Rome, where he was put in an iron chain in the year 38. But Caligula, already emperor for a year and used to his new powers, dramatically stated that he would exchange Agrippa's iron chain for a gold one. He had him released and gave him the lands formerly owned by his two uncles, Philip and Antipas, which Agrippa immediately went home to Palestine to claim.

Three years later, Caligula was assassinated by his bodyguard. Agrippa happened to be in Rome at the time and, hedging his bets, supported Claudius for emperor. When Claudius was chosen, he duly rewarded Agrippa by giving him Samaria and Judea and the title of king. Thus all the lands of his grandfather, Herod the Great, were now his. The Herodian kingdom was again restored, after having been divided up since 6 BCE.

Persecutions

By the year 40, Christianity (still considered a sect within Judaism) was established in many parts of the Roman Empire. The "good news" had been taken to Damascus, Antioch, Phoenicia, Cyprus, Greece, and elsewhere. In Palestine, Christian communities had sprung up in Samaria, in Galilee, in the Batanea east of the Jordan, and in the Decapolis. Many in these towns had known Jesus. According to Julius Africanus, part of his family lived in Kochaba in the Batanea.

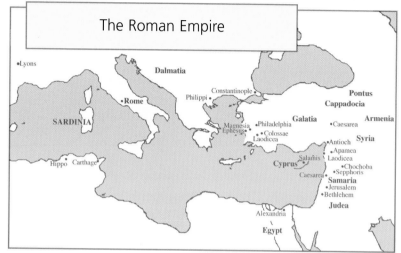

The Book of the Bee is a Nestorian Christian sacred history. It relates that the apostle James, the son of Zebedee and brother of John, was "spreading the gospel in Bethsaida." Agrippa took James prisoner, had him taken to Jerusalem and decapitated. We do not know what the charges were against him. Perhaps it was just stirring up trouble in a town that had been specifically dedicated to the cult of the Roman empress (now a goddess), Julia, by Philip Herod. James had been especially close to Jesus, was one of his very first disciples, and was with him at all the peak moments of his public career. The Gospels point out that he had expected to be rewarded with a special position at Jesus' right hand! It must have gone much against the grain for James to see a Roman goddess (and one whose life had been tainted) honored in his beloved town. He, who had listened to every word of Jesus, could not be silent.

In his third book of *Outlines,* Clement of Alexandria reports that the man who brought James into court was so moved when he saw him testify that he confessed that he, too, was a Christian: "So they were both taken away together, and on the way he asked James to forgive him. James thought for a moment; then he said 'I wish you peace' and kissed him. So both were beheaded at the same time."

The beautiful Armenian Church of Saint James is said to have been built on the place where James the apostle was buried. It is just a stone's throw from Mount Zion.

James was from the "inner circle," the brother of John. The execution of their close friend and colleague must have sent shocks of fear through the community. Did the enemies of this growing sect rejoice? The Acts of the Apostles reports that the murder of James so pleased certain of the Jews that Agrippa put Peter in jail, too (Acts 12:3), intending to execute him. But in this Agrippa would fail. Peter mysteriously disappeared. Agrippa had a search made for him, and, not finding him, had the prison guards put to death in his place. All subjects lived and died by the whim of the king. No one knew who would be next.

Peter, meanwhile, went to the house of Mary, the mother of John Mark, where Hellenistic believers were gathered in prayer for Passover. Since it was a pilgrim feast, doubtless many of the people of the Lord were present in Jerusalem. Rhoda, the serving girl, was so astonished to see Peter that she missed opening the door and ran to give the news to Mary's household! Peter told the group who were gathered in prayer to "report to James and the brothers." The fact that Peter went to Mary's house suggests that it was his house church. James must have belonged to a different house. After that Peter left for "another place" (Acts 12:17). Luke does not tell us where Peter went, but it may have been to Rome, where he was joined later on by John Mark. He is not met again in Acts until the Council of Jerusalem, several years later.

It is hardly surprising to read that with the departure of Peter, many members of the Greek-speaking church dispersed since Agrippa surely would not hesitate to take revenge on them. Eusebius tells that "the remaining apostles, in constant danger of murderous plots, were driven out of Jerusalem." This must have considerably narrowed the numbers left in the mother church.

Agrippa's palace at Caesarea Philippi

Leadership Passes to James

It was around the year 42 that James, the brother of Jesus, became the sole leader of the church in Jerusalem, which was made up almost entirely now of Aramaic-speaking Jewish Christians. Perhaps it was his outstanding piety, adherence to Jewish customs and laws, and constant attendance at the Temple that put him beyond the suspicion of Agrippa.

James was highly esteemed among the community and was known as the "righteous one." According to the apocryphal gospel of Thomas, when Jesus is asked, "Where are we going after you?" he replies, "Go to James." James became the one to be consulted. Jerusalem was the center to which those who had taken the message out to the nations returned to report. Thus his position was a most important one at this vital time.

James did not have to fear Agrippa for too long. In the spring of 44, Agrippa was in Caesarea by the sea, where he was to settle a dispute with a delegation from Tyre and Sidon. Josephus describes him as being adorned with magnificent royal robes, made entirely of silver. Mounted on the steps of the theater overlooking the turquoise Mediterranean, the king delivered a talk that the audience received with great applause. The morning sun caught the silver robe and it glistened. Those who looked on him were dazzled and hailed him as a god. Agrippa raised his hands and then, overcome with stomach ache, fell to the floor. He writhed in agony for five days and then died.

Because Agrippa's son was too young to take over, the land was once again put under Roman rule with Cuspius Fadus as procurator. Fadus was under the supervision of Cassius Longinus, governor of Syria.

The Jerusalem community must have breathed a sigh of relief. The Herod family would not be a threat, at least for a few years yet.

James as *Megaqqer*

But James had a difficult and dangerous role to play. While proclaiming the same message as had Peter, James was loyal to the Jewish law, the bulwark to preserve Jewish belief and the Jewish way of life. He became the *megaqqer*, the superintendent of the Jewish believers, a term that the first community likely took directly from the Essene establishment and meaning "bishop." *The Damascus Document* from Qumran states:

> The Megaqqer, superintendent, who is over all the camp, shall be from thirty to fifty years old, proficient in every council of men, and in every tongue according to their number. According to his direction those who enter the congregation shall enter, each in his turn. And any word which any man has to speak he shall speak to the Megaqqer concerning any controversy and decision.

The *megaqqer's* position required wisdom, prudence, diplomacy, understanding, and a great deal of courage, as well as piety.

Scholars often raise the question as to whether James was proficient in languages, since the Letter of James was written in Greek and James's native tongue was Aramaic. Doubtless as a builder at Nazareth (possibly working at Sepphoris) he had picked up some Greek. But, as *megaqqer* he certainly would have had access to Greek-speakers, especially among the Essenes. It is possible that one of his friends was Thabuti the Essene. This mysterious man is mentioned only twice in literature, once by Josephus and once by Eusebius, but he may have been a leader among the Essene priests who came over to belief in Jesus, and became chief assistant to James. We shall read more about him later.

Liturgy and Worship

The new community attended the synagogue, where the Torah and the Prophets were read on the Sabbath, but they had their own special messianic interpretation of these texts. (John Chrysostom tells that some ordinary Christians were attending both synagogue and church in his day, the end of the fourth century.) They developed their liturgy, concentrating on the death and resurrection of Jesus. It is probable that James often presided, although Essene priests may also have been in charge. How strong was the Essene influence in their liturgy and worship? In Judea, the Essene way must surely have influenced the life of the Jewish-Christian community.

They fasted on Wednesday and Friday (as did the Essenes) and celebrated the resurrection of Jesus on Sunday. The *Didache* says, "Do not fast like the hypocrites fast on Monday and Thursday, but fast on Wednesday and Friday" (the days when Jesus was taken prisoner and when he was crucified). It is quite likely that the practice of the Jerusalem church was the basis and model for other communities in the Diaspora. Wednesdays and Fridays are still days of fast in the Orthodox Church.

The community seems to have celebrated all the feasts of Judaism, but with reference to Jesus the Messiah. Passover, which was celebrated on the fourteenth of Nissan, had taken on new significance. The Nazoreans observed a fast during the Jewish hours of celebration of the Passover. It was only after midnight that the feast began for them. For Jews, the paschal lamb was to be eaten before midnight. For Jewish Christians, the meal was partaken after midnight but the ritual included commentary on the Passover narrative of the deliverance from Egypt. And for them the lamb indicated Christ. The pilgrim Melito of Sardis gives us to understand that the celebration went on until three o'clock in the morning. The Jewish expectation was that the Messiah would come on the night of Passover, as at the Exodus. Melito of Sardis in his *Paschal Sermons* suggests that Christians were hoping for the parousia in the middle of the night.

This Jewish-Christian rite became known as the Quartodecimans rite. When a gentile bishop was appointed in Caesarea after 135, the celebration was moved to the Sunday after the fourteenth of Nisan. It would become a contentious point later at the Council of Nicea, when Easter would supplant it.

Pentecost soon became the main feast, with the renewal of the New Covenant. This day had long been associated with newness: new bread and wine made from the new crop. At the start of Passover all the old bread was taken away and burned and the bread that was used after Passover until Pentecost was made from barley. For Passover they swung sheaves of barley before the altar, and for Pentecost, sheaves of new wheat. For the Essenes it was the day for the reception of new members into the community after a period of catechumenate. For the new Jewish Christians it was the day that commemorated the gift of the Holy Spirit.

Under Roman rule, the Temple priests' garments were kept locked up in the Fortress Antonia and a tax was charged to have them released at feast days. But in the year 45, an edict of Claudius allowed the Jews to keep the priestly garments in the Temple.

The position of high priest was assiduously sought after. As long as Agrippa II was a youth, his uncle Herod of Calcis was given the right to appoint the high priest. In 47, he appointed a brutal man, Ananias. Paul later called him a "white washed wall" and accused him of breaking the law that he was sworn to uphold by striking an accused prisoner who stood before him (Acts 23:2). The Jewish Christians, some of whom worshiped at the Temple, could expect little sympathy from such as him.

Tensions

There were many apprehensions within the community itself, especially as reports began to trickle in concerning what was happening in the spreading of the gospel in distant places. At Antioch, where followers of Jesus were called Christians for the first time (Acts 11:126), the message was catching on with unexpected speed. This city became the center for Hellenistic believers.

The Antiocheans did not conform to the rules. (Tacitus implies that *Christiani* was a term applied by the Romans to some troublemakers.) They did not insist on circumcision when accepting new gentile converts, as had been the practice for all converts to Judaism in former years. This was worrisome to pious Jews who believed that their faith was being diluted by the presence of gentiles, who also ignored dietary laws. James and the elders sent Barnabas to check on what was happening. But Barnabas became a prominent proponent of the liberal attitude and even went to Tarsus to find Paul to help him evangelize. They both taught in Antioch for a year. From Antioch, Paul and Barnabas undertook the first missionary journey between 45 and 49 (Acts 13:1ff), and this would bring new problems with it. When preaching to the Jews in Asia Minor, the two found themselves opposed by many orthodox Jews and decided to turn to the gentiles. They were convinced that gentiles could accept Christian baptism and faith in Christ without having to go through a Jewish conversion rite.

Often overlooked is that there was active Jewish proselytism going on as well. Josephus relates that John Hyrcanus forcibly circumcised the Idumaeans under threat of expulsion; later Aristobulus did the same to the Ituraeans; Alexander Janneus adopted the same policy in cities that he conquered. Marriage to a non-Jew required the other's conversion. Philo of Alexandria says of the Mosaic Law, "the whole of humanity might benefit from it and be guided towards a better life" (*Vita Mosis* 2 36f), and explains that there are "preachers in public places delivering the message of the Torah and delighting the minds of the hearer" (*Spec. Leg.* 1 320f). According to the census done under Claudius in 42 CE there were eight million Jews. Two million of these lived in Palestine; the rest were dispersed in various parts of the Roman Empire (Baron, *Social and Religious History of the Jews*). Matthew's Gospel has Jesus proclaim, "Woe to you scribes and Pharisees, hypocrites! for you cross sea and land to make a single convert" (23:15).

The people around James thought that this system of proselytism must continue. They

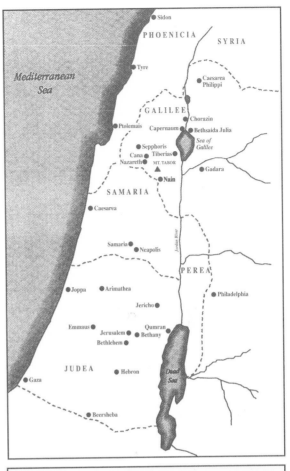

The land of Jesus

stressed the point that the covenant with God must be kept in its entirety. The gentiles must be encouraged to keep the law of Moses. Their argument was that Jesus was circumcised and had obeyed the law of Moses. Believers in Jesus must do the same.

But Barnabas and Paul, who had experience out in the world, saw that such an attitude would hinder the acceptance of the gospel by the gentiles. At the end of the decade matters came to a head. The community of Antioch decided to send a delegation to Jerusalem to get the response of James and the apostles on this subject of vital importance. Paul and Barnabas had to have their praxis examined by the council. They set out for Jerusalem, going by foot through Phoenicia and Samaria to get the grassroots support of these communities. At the report of the conversion of the gentiles and their acceptance of Jesus, "there was great joy" in these communities.

News of this mission must have spread. Upon reaching Jerusalem they were received by James and the apostles, who were gathered at Mount Zion. Peter and the others had returned to settle the question of the reception of Gentiles, and the first council of the church took place in 48.

Council of Jerusalem

The predominant question was the integration of the gentiles into the church. The leaders came from afar to discuss the issue. We do not know how long it took before a quorum was present in Jerusalem or where they stayed. Peter had left Jerusalem in 42 and had been away for over six years. Had he had contact with the others during that time? Paul must have had some apprehension about seeing again those with whom he had collaborated in the persecution of Christians in his early years. We know that when he returned again in 57, he would have trouble with leading Jews.

As the council commenced, some believers who belonged to the Pharisee element insisted that new converts be circumcised as well as baptized. The group around Paul and Barnabas maintained that acceptance of Jesus as the Messiah and faith in him were sufficient to receive them into the church.

After vehement arguments, Peter took the floor and spoke, arguing that in his personal experience in the conversion of Cornelius, God himself had made the decision. Peter had noticed that after speaking of the Lord to them, the Holy Spirit came down upon Cornelius and his household just as they themselves had received the Spirit as Jews. Since God had spoken so clearly, he had decided to baptize those gentiles without preliminary circumcision. So now, too, he maintained that faith should be the only requirement. And he added an argument from experience. "Now, therefore, why are you putting God to the test by placing on the necks of the disciples a yoke that neither our ancestors nor we have been able to bear?" (Acts 15:10).

Did Peter realize that by saying so he was splitting the community of believers into a group that was bound to the covenant of Moses, and those that knew only the new covenant, the cross and resurrection of Jesus Christ? The community must have been astounded at the daring of this proposal. They kept silent. They were astonished that something like this was possible. With admiration, and with great expectations, they listened while Barnabas and Paul related their story. And now everyone was anxious to hear the response of James, the brother of the Lord, of Davidic descent, head of the church in Jerusalem.

His word was of tremendous import. To the surprise of the Jewish believers he agreed with the statement of Peter. He added his decisive voice, supporting the position of Paul and Barnabas (Acts 15:13–21). There was only one covenant and that is the covenant of Moses, and Jesus was part of it. God himself has decided, in our days, with the coming of Jesus, to make out of the gentiles a people for his name. He cited Amos:

> "After this I will return, and rebuild the dwelling of David which has fallen; from its ruins I will rebuild it and I will set it up, so that all other people may seek the Lord. Even all the Gentiles over whom my name has

been called. Thus says the Lord who has been making these things known from long ago." (Acts 15:16–18)

There is hardly any doubt that James wanted to impress on his listeners the fact that the prophecy had finally found fulfillment in Jesus his brother. It is interesting that what Amos said of the house of David (Amos 9:11–15), James extended to all the nations:

> Therefore I have reached the decision that we should not trouble those Gentiles who are turning to God, but we should write to them to abstain only from things polluted by idols and from fornication and from whatever has been strangled and from blood. For in every city, for generations past, Moses has had those who proclaim him, for he has been read aloud every sabbath in the synagogues. (Acts 15:19–21)

So the head of the community agreed with Simon Peter that God had elected a people out of the gentiles that was not bound to circumcision and the law of Moses. But James, steeped in Jewish tradition, insisted on certain conditions: new converts were required "to abstain from things polluted by idols, and from fornication and from whatever has been strangled and from blood." (How to slaughter was important to the ancients. If the blood was still there, the life was still there. Originally, all slaughtering was a sacrifice.)

But he has a word of consolation for those who were loyal to him and to the covenant of Moses. "For in every city, for generations past, Moses has had those who proclaim him for he has been read aloud every sabbath in the synagogues." Thus he applied a plaster dressing to the wound. It seems to have quieted them for a while, but it did not effect healing.

The community then sent Judas called Barsabas and Silas, among others, to convey the message to Antioch. They sent a letter as well, which unfortunately has not been preserved.

FAMINE

The year 47 to 48 was a sabbatical year. Every obedient Jew let the land lie fallow. Since we know that in the next year there was a famine in the Empire, one indeed wonders whether the sabbatical may have contributed to the famine, which started in 48. We learn from Josephus (*Antiq.* xx, ii, 6) that Queen Helena of Adiabene, a Jewish proselyte, helped the population of Jerusalem. The new gentile group at Antioch also supported them. How well the "community of goods" fared at this time, we do not know.

Death of Mary

An old Jerusalem Jewish-Christian tradition, the *Transitus Mariae*, tells that at this time, Mary, the mother of Jesus, was living on Mount Zion in the house of John and of James. The *Protoevangelium of James* tells that "James loved Mary very much." Although we hear nothing of her activity, she must have been the heart of the family.

According to various manuscripts of the *Transitus Mariae*, Mary died at the time of the council when the apostles were in Jerusalem. She would have been more than seventy years old. A beautiful icon in the crypt of Dormition Abbey imagines the scene. Mary, surrounded by the loving friends of her son, falls asleep and is taken at once to be held in the arms of Jesus, just as she must have held him as a baby. Not far away, just by the garden of Gethsemane, the Orthodox Christians venerate the tomb of Mary. Legend tells that Thomas was not present for the burial of Mary, but was later taken to her burial place by the apostles. They found the tomb empty but it was filled with flowers.

Icon of the Dormition (death or "falling asleep") of Mary

This passing of the mother of Jesus, the one who had been closest to him, was a time of great sadness. Her presence among them surely had been a solidifying one. For James, this woman had been his caretaker and mentor since childhood. Now her loving presence was gone.

Troubles for James

The year 49 would be a memorable one for James. After the Council of Jerusalem we hear no more of Peter or of the other apostles. In 1 Corinthians 9, Paul implies that all of them and the brethren of Jesus (together with their wives) were involved in proselytizing in the eastern Mediterranean. James was sole leader of the original church.

In 49 the zealots, never quite predictable, were making their presence known in the Diaspora and causing insurgence. Claudius expelled the Jews from Rome. The ripples from this wave must have reached Jerusalem.

Writing

By this time, what was being written? Possibly Mary kept the tradition of the birth and youth of Jesus alive. We can only speculate that her stories were written down, perhaps by a member of the family. Paul and Mark knew nothing about them, but later they became the source of the Gospel stories of Jesus' childhood. About the year 48, as those who had known Jesus were beginning to die, the oral tradition of the gospel may have begun to be put into written form. Scholars believe that an Aramaic form of Matthew's Gospel was put together at this time. Perhaps the sayings of Jesus were written down. Did James start a commentary, which would eventually be his letter, right after the Council of Jerusalem? This letter takes a stand quite different to Paul's on the relationship of faith to "good works." And the letters of Paul were beginning to circulate. In the winter of 49, Paul was in Corinth and wrote his first letter to the Thessalonians.

Soon after the Council of Jerusalem, Barnabas and Paul, who had come back to Antioch, wanted to embark on another journey. But a quarrel arose about the reliability of John Mark (the nephew of Barnabas), who had deserted them in Cyprus, and Barnabas and Paul parted.

Was the nephew of Barnabas the one who wrote the Gospel of Mark? He is as likely a candidate as any. Mark became the interpreter of Peter when Paul dismissed him. Peter went to Rome. Did Mark start writing his Gospel then? He was very well versed in the events around Jesus and might even have known him. While scholars agree that his Gospel was produced in about the year 70, there is evidence that he started his compilation earlier.

Meanwhile, in 48, the son of Agrippa II and great-grandson of Herod the Great came of age, and the Herods would once again head the land of the Jews.

CHAPTER THREE

PROBLEMS ADAPTING TO GENTILES
THE YEARS 50–60

In Rome in the year 50, Claudius was emperor. The strong-willed Quamandus Ummidius governed the province of Syria. In Judea, the procurator was the Quadrates Comanus, an impetuous man. The territory of Gaulinitis and Lysanias in northern Palestine had been given by Claudius to young Agrippa II when the latter attained his majority.

The Empire was at peace, but all was not quiet. Insurrections were frequent but were dealt with swiftly and severely.

In Palestine, the Jews and Samaritans had had an unhealthy relationship stretching back for centuries. Early in 52, some Galileans on their way to Jerusalem were killed by Samaritans. Mobs of frenzied Jews invaded Samaria. In typical Roman fashion, the procurator sought to quell the conflict by sending in his cavalry. Many on both sides were killed or imprisoned. The Samaritans sent a message to the Syrian governor, who happened to be in Jerusalem, and the governor ordered the crucifixion of the Jewish prisoners. The procurator, however, sided with the Jews. The governor settled the question by sending the procurator to Rome, where he was banished by Claudius. Antonius Felix, a former slave, was appointed in his place. We read his name several times in the Acts of the Apostles.

Felix was a man with panache who did not let his lowly background stand in his way. He lost no time in establishing himself. Commitments meant little to him. His first act upon arriving in the territory was to persuade Drusilia, the sister of Agrippa, to divorce her husband Azizus, king of Emesa, and marry him. He had a propensity for collecting wives, and he married several times (one of his wives was the granddaughter of Anthony and Cleopatra). A man of the world, he was not above being bribed. And he was "rather well informed about the new way" (Acts 24:22). Paul was tried before him. Later, he used to send for Paul frequently to converse with him over the two-year period of Paul's imprisonment in Caesarea. Felix was procurator from 52 until he was recalled in 59, and is remembered by the historian Tacitus as "a prime example of mismanagement."

The half-crazed Nero became emperor of Rome in 54. In 55 he added the territory of Galilee and Perea to the domain of Agrippa, thus giving him almost all of the land his grandfather had ruled (except for Judea), and bestowed on him the title of king. Being deprived of Judea must have been a disappointment to the young man, but as a consolation prize he was given the Hasmonean royal

Model of Jerusalem Temple: Entrance of the Holy of Holies

palace in Jerusalem, which gave him the right to appoint the high priest. Immediately he nominated the youngest son of Annas, Ananus, to the position. Of old, the position of high priest called for men of the highest caliber and learning, but since the Herod family had assumed responsibility for making the appointment, its occupants were men of cupidity and lust for power who bribed their way to it.

Palestine was suffering an economic depression. By now the reconstruction of the Temple was completed and there was much unemployment. Agrippa initiated a public works program of paving the streets and mending the roads that led into Jerusalem, which were in bad repair. Heavy taxes were levied on people who were scarcely eking out a living, and they caused great bitterness. Casual day workers vied with one another for employment. Frequent fights erupted. It would take only a small spark to ignite a fire.

The fire happened at Passover in 55, when a Roman soldier made a vulgar gesture to the crowd gathered for prayer. A riot broke out; "30, 000 were crushed to death," Josephus recalls, and there was "bereavement in every household." Even allowing for Josephus' occasional tendency to exaggerate, a large number must have been killed. Josephus recalls, too, that a quarrel broke out between the chief priests and the leaders of the Jerusalem populace. Both sides recruited ruffians to aid them, and when they met they threw stones at one another. "The scandal went on with impunity as though in a city without a government." The high priest, who was one of the richest men in the city, sent slaves to seize the tithes from the Temple on which the lower-class priests depended, and destitute priests perished from want.

Church of St. Peter in Gallicantu ("Cock Crow") and steps to house of Caiaphas, where Jesus may have walked

A new type of bandit sprang up, the *sicarii*. Their favorite trick was to mingle with festive crowds, concealing under their garments small daggers with which they stabbed their opponents and then melted into the throng. Bandits were everywhere, and highwaymen hid out on the roads ready to pounce on innocent travelers. Felix tried to clear up the outlaws, putting down, as Josephus records, "the robbers and the imposters" who "were a multitude not to be enumerated." And he was not above using the services of the *sicarii* to cut the throat of Jonathan the high priest. "This caused fear among the people, who every day expected death as in war." Terrorism was widespread.

Community of Goods

How did the community of goods in Jerusalem survive economically? The story of Ananias and Sapphira (Acts 5:1–11) implies that it was not functioning too well. Some were holding back their share. The Letter of James, which may have been written at this time, speaks of troubles in the community and refers often to the blessings of the poor. Paul brought a collection to Jerusalem in 56–57, suggesting that there was monetary need. But the idea of sharing all in common seems to have continued until the flight to Pella in the late 60s.

Covenants

The situation was far from serene on Mount Zion for reasons other than economic. Fierce loyalty to Jewish law and traditions was felt here. Josephus describes James as "strict in the observance of the law." The solution reached at the Council of Jerusalem to admit gentiles without circumcision was a pragmatic one, and James went along with it on condition that the Jews continued to observe their covenant, which required circumcision and observance of the Mosaic Law. They were, after all, the Chosen People. The gentiles were persons with whom God, on account of the merit of the God-man Jesus Christ, had made a new covenant. This new covenant was that God saves humankind not through their deeds but by faith in the death and resurrection of our Lord. James recognized two covenants, the covenant of Moses that applied to themselves as Jews, and the covenant of Jesus, which applied to Jews and gentiles.

THE AGAPE

There was much interior tension concerning the community of the table, the "Agape." Could gentiles eat together with circumcised Jews? This was a question that remained open and was particularly relevant in Antioch. After Paul and Barnabas had returned to Antioch, they were very happy to announce the decision of the Council of Jerusalem. But doubts remained. Could Jews that observed the law have table community with gentiles? When Peter visited Antioch he ate with pagans, but when people came from James they insisted on separation and Peter ate separately. He felt bound to keep a separate table, or let himself be persuaded into this way of doing things. Apparently he had consulted with Barnabas, who, after some doubt, agreed with him.

Paul became enraged. He started to shout at Peter. He contended that the conversion of the gentiles was not being taken seriously, and the fellowship of the community was being destroyed. Paul felt very deeply about the matter, jumped into the middle of the assembly, and provoked an uproar, accusing people of not being completely honest. Why should they not be able to eat together? Were dietary laws more important than love and friendship? The two groups never solved it. This outbreak of fury was divisive and soon after, Paul split with Barnabas. They did not question the Eucharist, but simply the agape. In Jerusalem itself this would have been a non-issue since all were Jewish. Nonetheless, reports were being sent back to James. Coping with change was not easy.

Writings

We see in this decade the beginning of the writings that would later be incorporated into the scriptures. Paul's letters were written from various parts of the Empire. Scholars say that the Gospel of Mark may have been put into primitive form at this time. Eusebius gives an account of what happened with the arrival of Peter in Rome: "Clad in divine armor, like a noble captain of God, he brought the precious merchandise of the spiritual light from the East to those in the West, preaching the good news of light itself and the soul saving word." He goes on to say that the enthusiastic crowd asked for more and wanted more than oral teaching. "They asked Mark, a follower of Peter, to leave them in writing a summary of the instructions they had received by word of mouth, nor did they let him go until they had persuaded him, and thus became responsible for the writing of what is known as the Gospel of Mark." Clement of Rome in his *Outlines* quotes the story that, on learning by revelation of the spirit what had happened, Peter was delighted at their enthusiasm, and ordered the reading of the book in the churches.

It is not possible to definitely identify any of the writers of the four canonical Gospels. Mark was a very common name in the Roman Empire. It is most frequently thought that the author of Mark's Gospel was the young man mentioned in the Acts of the Apostles who was the cousin of Barnabas and had deserted him and Paul in Cyprus. This Mark was an interpreter for Peter. The Gospel is written in Greek. The Mark mentioned in the Acts of the Apostles knew Greek well; because he had been brought up in a Hellenistic family it was his first language. He had heard the traditions of Jesus repeated again and again and may even have known Jesus personally.

Many believe that it was at this time that the sayings of Jesus, now referred to as "Q" (from the German word *quelle* for "source"), were put together, although the provenance of this collection is unknown. Mark did not know about the existence of "Q" or the infancy narrative. Mark was no longer living in Jerusalem, and had probably left there fairly early on. Tradition has it that he eventually went to Egypt.

The Letter of James

It took many centuries for the Letter of James to be accepted as canonical. While some modern scholars opt for pseudonymity—that an anonymous author wrote the letter and attributed it to James of Jerusalem—many others believe that it originated in Jerusalem and that James the *Tzadik*, the brother of the Lord, was its author. We see in the primitive church two currents of thought concerning the centrality of faith. On the extreme right stood James with his conservative attitude toward the Law of Moses, and on the extreme left, Paul. Paul's position was of free faith independent of the Law of Moses. Faith in Jesus was sufficient for salvation. The Letter of James speaks to all the members of the twelve tribes that had become believers through circumcision, especially those living in Palestine and the surrounding regions like Syria and Egypt. It is addressed to Jews who had accepted Christ. The frequent references to the Bible suppose that those texts were of common knowledge to his readers. The style used is not of a letter, but is rather of a homily with exhortation, as it was done at Jewish religious services in the synagogue.

Two basic themes can be noticed in this letter. The first theme exalts the poor and has strong reservations and warnings toward the wealthy. The author's sympathy goes toward the marginalized and the *anawim*. These are the darlings of God. James draws from the ancient biblical traditions but more especially from the spirit expressed in the Sermon on the Mount.

The second theme stresses the importance of good deeds and warns against unfruitful faith. "Be doers of the word and not merely hearers who deceive themselves." Raymond Brown suggests that James is correcting a misunderstanding of the Pauline formula. "Paul was arguing that observance of ritual works prescribed by the Mosaic Law, particularly circumcision, would not justify the gentiles; faith in what God had done in Christ was required—a faith that involved a commitment of life."

The theme of a religion of action is important and occurs in other New Testament writings: "And everyone who hears the words of mine and does not act on them will be like a foolish man who built his house on sand" (Matt 7:26), and "My mother and my brothers are those who hear the word of God and do it" (Luke 8:21).

What is surprising in the letter (and the reason why many question its having been written by James of Jerusalem) is such excellent Greek! Could it be that one of the very learned Essenes assisted James in formulating this letter? Thabuti is mentioned only peripherally in the literature but may have had a very important role. He is certainly a likely candidate to be James' assistant and the writer of this letter. Robert Eisenman, a scholar of the Dead Sea Scrolls, has this to say: "The Letter of James in its essence resembles nothing so much as the Dead Sea Scrolls, which is why, prior to their discovery, it may have been difficult to appreciate it."

Possibly it was put together in Greek by one who had also participated in the writing of the scrolls, such as Thabuti.

The Position of James

The Letter of James, addressed to Jews in the Diaspora, suggests that Jewish Christians consulted him. The primacy of the church in Jerusalem is attested to in the Acts of the Apostles by the decisions made at the Council of Jerusalem, and by James sending messengers to Antioch to approve their reception of converts. Indeed, Paul in the Letter to the Galatians refers to James as a pillar of the church (Gal 2:9).

Confrontation

In the summer of 57 Paul returned to Jerusalem (Acts 21:17ff), and a very important meeting took place. Paul came with a gift of money for the community, which he had been collecting in Greece and in Asia Minor (Rom 15:25ff). When he arrived in Caesarea, Agabus, who had just come from Judea, warned him not to go to Jerusalem, since they "will hand him over to the Gentiles." But Paul refused to listen, and said he was willing not only to be imprisoned, but also to die for the name of Jesus.

There were thousands of believing Jews by now living in the city. It was Paul's intention to help in a material way those from whom the word had first gone out. He also wanted to be in Jerusalem for Pentecost:

> At present, however, I am going to Jerusalem in a ministry to the saints; for Macedonia and Achaia have been pleased to share their resources with the poor among the saints at Jerusalem. They were pleased to do this, and indeed they owe it to them; for if the Gentiles have come to share in their spiritual blessings, they ought also to be of service to them in material things…join me in earnest prayer to God on my behalf, that I may be rescued from the unbelievers in Judea, and that my ministry to Jerusalem may be acceptable to the saints. (Rom 15:25ff)

Paul, a generous spirit, was obviously apprehensive about this visit to Jerusalem. He would have to cope not only with nonbelieving Jews in Jerusalem because of his activity in not requiring circumcision of converts, but also with how well he would be received by believing Jews.

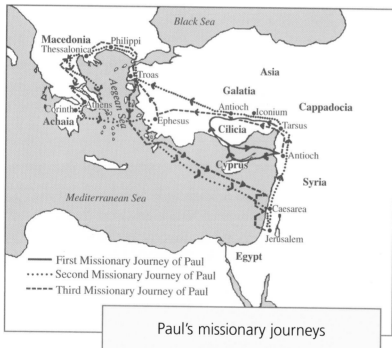

First Missionary Journey of Paul
Second Missionary Journey of Paul
Third Missionary Journey of Paul

Paul's missionary journeys

Circumcision had a long and important history among the Jews. At the time of the Greeks, many had died rather than not have their sons circumcised. Circumcision was their distinctive mark and Paul was accused of belittling it: "You teach all the Jews living among the Gentiles, to forsake Moses, and that you tell them not to circumcise their children" (Acts 21:21).

The day after he arrived, Paul went to see James and the elders to hand over his gift. One can imagine the uneasy scene. On the one side of the room were Paul and his companions from Caesarea, and on the other, the entire assembly of Jewish believers. Paul enthusiastically announced to them the good news of his success among the gentiles and his activity found full approval. They "glorified God." His work among the gentiles was paralleled by their work among the Jews, of whom ten thousand (a myriad) had become believers and were loyal to the Law of Moses.

The authorities in Jerusalem deferred to the position taken at the Council of Jerusalem (Acts 15:20) that gentiles should be put under no undue difficulties. Now, after some thirty years after the death of Christ, there were two divisions in the family, the traditional Jewish group, which remained inside Judaism adhering to the Mosaic Law and circumcision while professing baptism and belief in Jesus, and the new group, espousing faith in Christ and baptism and not requiring circumcision. They were able to look on success beyond all expectations. Both groups had accepted their different positions.

But then James went on to say that reports had reached them about Paul not requiring Jews to observe the law any longer: "You teach all the Jews living among the gentiles to forsake Moses."

The many Jews in Jerusalem who had become believers were disturbed by this report that came in from Asia Minor through nonbelieving Jews. Paul was being accused of trying to get the Diaspora to give up the Mosaic laws, and this excited many. James himself wanted to be a pious Jew, loyal to the law, and he expected the same from the others.

James took the floor to announce that there was no problem on the part of the believing Jews. Danger came only from the nonbelieving Jews:

> You see, brothers, how many thousands of believers there are among the Jews and they are all zealous for the law. They have been told about you that you teach all the Jews living among the Gentiles to forsake Moses, and that you tell them not to circumcise their children, or observe the customs. What then is to be done? They will certainly hear that you have come. (Acts 21:20–22)

James then proposed that Paul overcome these false accusations by an action that would show him as a loyal Jew.

Did James judge Paul's position correctly? First it must be said that Paul never had influenced Jews to apostatize from the law. We know from his letter to the Galatians that he justifies the gospel of the circumcised beside the gospel to the noncircumcised (Gal 2:7–9). To be Christian and Jew is not necessarily incompatible. His Jewish foes had misrepresented his doctrine that circumcision does not justify by itself. The only thing that Paul expected from Jewish Christians was that, despite their observance of the law and their Jewish way of life, they would have a brotherly communion with those believers who were gentiles (Gal 2:11). He became for the gentiles a gentile and for the Jews, a Jew (1 Cor 9:19ff). He had Timothy circumcised out of sensitivity to the Jews (Acts 16:3). He went to Jerusalem for the feasts. He visited the Temple whenever he could. He kept the feast days of the Jews so he could also take part in their rituals of purification. He was proud of his Jewish origins and upbringing (Rom 9:3ff, 11:1; 2 Cor 11:22; and Phil 3:5).

James suggested that he overcome the enmity of the nonbelievers by having him join the four Jewish-Christian men who had taken the Nazarite vow, purify himself with them, and carry the expenses for the required sacrifice. By doing so James hoped that Paul would overcome the bad feeling of the Jewish Christians against him. He also stressed that the relationship to the gentile Christians had already been regulated in the Council of Jerusalem.

Paul decided to follow the suggestion of James because by doing so he would express that he was no enemy or despiser of Jewish prescriptions. Taking the Nazarite vow could take up to thirty days. Details of the custom are obscure. During the thirty days, the vow-takers were not allowed to cut their hair; they had to visit the Temple and offer up a sacrifice, and when their hair was cut it was put in the fire of the sacrifice (Num 6:13ff). They also offered

> One male lamb, a year old without blemish, as a burnt offering, one yew lamb, a year old without blemish, as a sin offering, one ram without blemish, as an offering of well-being, and a basket of unleavened bread, cakes of choice flour mixed with oil, and unleavened wafers spread with oil, and their grain offering and their drink offering.

The cost was considerable and could not be borne by many. It was the custom that the wealthy would pay for the poor, and this was considered a good work.

Besides taking on himself the expense of the sacrifice, Paul had a ritual bath with the four men so as to be able to eat the meal with them in purity. In the Jewish culture, Jews who had been living in a foreign land and in constant contact with gentiles were in a state of impurity. Paul went through the rites of purification and then "entered the temple with them, making public the completion of the days of purification when the sacrifice would be made for each of them " (Acts 21:26).

It was in the Temple precincts that Jews who had come from Asia saw Paul, and they were angry. They stirred up the crowd, dragged Paul out of the Temple, and shut the gate. They accused him of spreading his teachings everywhere against the law, and even bringing gentiles into the Temple and profaning the sacred place. They would have killed him had not the Tribune, Lysias, seen what was going on from his room in the Antonia Fortress and sent soldiers down to investigate. They arrested Paul and had to carry him through the crowds because of the violence. Lysias was confused and thought that Paul might be the Egyptian who had recently led four hundred assassins in the wilderness. Josephus tells us that this Egyptian and his followers had been eradicated by a surprise attack by the procurator Felix on the Mount of Olives.

Paul was allowed to make a speech to the Jews and tell them about his conversion, but when he had finished they still called out to "rid the earth of this man." The Tribune prudently took him away for further examination, and now for the first time,

Paul told of his Roman citizenship and appealed to Caesar.

At Pentecost of 57, Paul was taken prisoner in the temple. He was brought before the Sanhedrin, where he set Pharisees against Sadducees by proclaiming, "I am on trial concerning the hope of the resurrection of the dead." An uproar ensued. Some from the Pharisee party were willing to set him free and this infuriated others. During the night forty Jews took a vow not to eat or drink until they had killed Paul. Fortunately Paul's nephew overheard them and went to the Roman commander, who had Paul taken to Caesarea.

At Caesarea Paul was tried before Felix. The High Priest Ananias came down to Caesarea and brought with him the attorney Tertullus to present the case for the elders (Acts 24:1–8). They contended that Paul was a pestilent fellow, "an agitator among all the Jews throughout the world...he even tried to profane the temple" (Acts 24:5–6). Paul acted as his own lawyer and so impressed Felix that the proconsul ordered him kept in custody but allowed freedom of movement and permitted his friends to care for his wants. From this time on, Paul was a prisoner. Felix came often to converse with him, hoping to be offered a bribe!

Palestine under early procurators

We have no evidence of James attempting to help Paul. From 57–59 Paul was in Caesarea. He was then presented to Festus (who had replaced Felix as procurator) and appealed to Rome. He made his defense in the presence of Agrippa II and his sister, Bernice, who took a liking to Paul. Perhaps he might have been set free had he never mentioned his Roman citizenship.

In the fall of 59, Paul was sent to Rome. He was shipwrecked in Malta, and stayed the winter there before proceeding to the eternal city, where he would eventually be beheaded.

Meanwhile, there is no evidence that the church in Jerusalem showed any interest during the two years that Paul was in Caesarea. Luke, who was his friend, does not mention any messengers being sent to him. Perhaps Paul was too controversial a figure for James to cope with. Would the Jewish community have been in jeopardy by trying to aid him?

Generous Paul, who had risked his life to come to the aid of the Jewish community, stood alone. The Jewish Christians did not know the man, just as Peter had denied knowing Jesus.

On the wall of the dungeon of the house of Caiaphas, where Jesus was held captive, the pilgrim today can see written in Latin the words *Non novi illum,* perhaps the greatest betrayal of all: "I do not know him."

CHAPTER FOUR

DEATH OF JAMES, HERESY, FLIGHT TO PELLA: THE YEARS 60–70

The ten years between 60 and 70 were marked by hostility within and without the emerging church. James was murdered. Simon Bar Cleophas was elected in his place, and the first heretical group appeared on the scene. In Rome, a persecution of Christians started at the time of the great fire in 64, and full-scale martyrdom ensued a few years later. Tacitus records what happened to these early Christians:

> They were put to death with exquisite cruelty, and to their suffering Nero added mockery and derision. Some were covered with skins of animals, and left to be devoured by dogs; others were nailed to crosses; numbers of them were burned alive; many, covered with inflammable matter, were set on fire to serve as torches during the night.

The Zealot rebellion started in Israel in 66 and resulted in the almost complete destruction of Jerusalem and the Temple and the creation of Rabbinic Judaism. The Jewish-Christian community itself abandoned Mount Zion and established itself elsewhere.

Nero ruled as emperor until 68 when he was forced to commit suicide. Two other emperors, Galba and Otto, followed in quick succession. Vespasian, the army general who would put down the

Bethsaida

Zealot rebellion in Palestine, would be established on the imperial throne by popular acclaim before the decade ended.

Syria had a series of short-lived governors: Cerbula held the governorship until 63, followed by Cestius Gallus, who governed until 66. Mucianus was governor in 67 and 68.

A Roman procurator continued in Judea. Festus held the position from 60 to 62. He died in office, and there was a hiatus between his death and the arrival of his successor, Albinus. (This lull was to be catastrophic for the Jewish community, as we shall see.) Albinus was procurator until 64. Then Florus took over the position from 64 to 66. (He was nominated by Poppaea, the beautiful and spoiled wife of Nero.)

During this decade, Agrippa II was king of all of Palestine except Judea but held the privilege of appointing the high priest. He appointed six between 58 and 64, all from the family of Ananus.

The Jewish-Christian group saw itself threatened by internal upheavals over which it had a measure of control, but also by political events over which it had none. The end of the decade would mark the end of the apostolic age, with most leaders who had known Jesus moved off the stage, most to meet death by martyrdom. Peter was crucified in Rome (tradition has it that the cross was placed upside down). Andrew died by crucifixion in Greece.

Paul had been sent to Rome by Festus after his appeal to the emperor. There, under military surveillance from the year 60 on, he used his time for apostolic work. People were free to visit him. He was a Roman citizen, a privilege that none of the other Christian leaders had. He would be martyred in Rome by beheading (Roman citizens were not crucified) in about the year 67.

Death of James

Eusebius tells us that when Paul was sent to Rome, his enemies turned their venom on the church in Jerusalem. Their attack on Paul had really been aimed at James, the head of the Jewish-Christian community, but his respectable lifestyle and his good reputation among the people prevented any action against him for a while. The opportunity arose at Easter of 62.

Festus had died and a new procurator was on his way to Judea. But before he arrived, the high priest, Ananus (whose father and four brothers had preceded him as high priest), planned an attack against James. Josephus describes Ananus as "a bold man in his temper, and very insolent." Bold indeed he was, and he succeeded in having James lynched.

This powerful man urged the Scribes and Pharisees to demand that James make a public declaration of his adherence to the Jewish faith through a gesture in the Temple. This was highly illegal. They stood him up on the parapet of the sanctuary of the Temple so that his words could be heard by all around. (A parapet was a low protective wall put around the roof to prevent people from falling.) Hegesippus claims that James showed "undreamed of fearlessness" in the face of the throng and instead gave a splendid sermon about Jesus, insisting that Jesus was the Son of God. Some among the

crowd were convinced by his words and began to chant, "Hosanna to the son of David." This further enraged the Scribes and Pharisees, who rushed at him and threw him off the parapet, a drop of some one hundred feet. They then went rushing down to see where he had fallen and, seeing that he was not dead from the fall, some began to stone him. A fuller took a club that he used to beat out clothes and brought it down forcefully on the victim's head.

Pinnacle of the Temple

The original intent was to have James decry Jesus. Now the body of this holy and highly respected man lay bludgeoned outside Judaism's holiest place. How shamefaced the leaders of the affair must have been! Josephus tells us that "many citizens were uneasy at the breach in the laws, and sent to the king Agrippa, desiring him to send to Ananus that he should act no more...and some of them went to meet Albinus and informed him that it was not lawful to assemble a sanhedrin without his consent...whereupon Albinus wrote in anger to Ananus...King Agrippa took the high priesthood from him when he had ruled but three months."

At the time of his death, James would have been about seventy years old. He had been greatly esteemed by all. Hegesippus claims:

> This one was holy from birth; he drank no wine or intoxicating liquor
> and ate no animal food; no razor came near his head; he did not smear
> himself with oil, and took no baths.

This latter may refer to taking no mikvah, as James had been baptized. Since the Essenes regularly undertook the mikvah, this suggests that, while associated with the Essenes, James was not himself an Essene:

He alone was permitted to enter the holy place, for his garments were not of wool but of linen [the Essenes wore linen as did priests]. He used to enter the sanctuary alone and was often found on his knees beseeching forgiveness for the people, so that his knees grew hard like camels from his continually bending them in worship of God.

Eusebius writes:

The chair of James, who was the first to receive from the Savior and his apostles the episcopacy of the Jerusalem church, and was called Christ's brother as the sacred books show, has been preserved to this day. There, Christians, who in their turn look after it with such loving care, make clear to all the veneration in which saintly men high in the favor of God were regarded in time past and are regarded this day.

The Ossuary of St. James?

The Tomb of James the *Tzadik*

James was buried close by the Temple in the valley of the Kidron in a burial garden where Hegesippus says his tomb was venerated even in his day (180 CE). An intriguing pericope in the Copper Scroll of the Essenes (a sort of treasure-hunt map) reads:

Below the corner of the Southern Portico of the Temple is the tomb of Sadok, under the pillar of the Exedron, vessels of tithe for soah…on the treading place at the top of the rock facing west against the garden of Sadok under the great stone slab of the water…

Since the tomb of "Sadok" was surrounded by a garden, it must have been maintained by a group who lived close by (on Mount Zion?). Could this be the burial place of James the *Tzadik*? Were the "Sadok" and the *"Tzadik"* the same person? Could the Copper Scroll be referring to the tomb of James, the brother of the Lord? If so, we have a definite connection with the Essene community. The recent finding of the ossuary with the inscription "James, son of Joseph, brother of Jesus" also is intriguing. Noted scholar Joseph Fitzmyer says that the spelling of the name James on the ossuary is unusual but is the same spelling of the name found in the Dead Sea Scrolls. And further, the word for "brother" is an unusual form but is found in the *Genesis Apocryphon* from Qumran Cave 1.

That James was held in high esteem is demonstrated by stories about him that survived the centuries. The medieval pilgrim Felix Fabri, writing in his journal in 1484, notes:

> To this cave, Saint James fled for refuge when the Lord was taken prisoner, and there he lay hid. We are told by Josephus and Jerome, in their lives of famous men, that when the Lord died upon the cross he vowed that he would not eat food until he should see the Lord risen from the dead; so on the day of the resurrection the Lord came into this cave to him and Himself gave him food. After the apostle's death his body was brought into this cave, and buried there; consequently from that time forth the place began to be venerated and resorted to by Christ's faithful people even to this day.

Felix was probably quoting from the diary of earlier pilgrims, as was usual with medieval journalers.

The Election of a Successor to James

After the death of James, the elective council got together to choose his successor. Eusebius reports:

> Those of the apostles and disciples of the Lord who were still living assembled from all parts, together with those who, humanely speaking, were kinsmen of the Lord, for most of those were still living. Then they all discussed together whom they should choose as a fit person to succeed James, and voted unanimously that Simon, son of the Cleophas mentioned in the gospel narrative, was a fit person to occupy the throne of the Jerusalem see. He was, so it is said, a cousin of the Savior.

Were Peter and John present at this council? Eusebius says that all of the apostles and disciples who were still alive came from all parts. It may well be that they wanted to see continuity in this community and regarded one who had known Jesus and was a Davidite as most qualified. It indicates too that the Jerusalem church was still regarded as of prime importance.

How was Simon related to Jesus? John's Gospel (19:25) talks of Mary, wife of Cleophas, standing by her sister, Mary, the mother of Jesus, at the foot of the cross. This would mean that Simon was related to Jesus not only through his father Cleophas (the

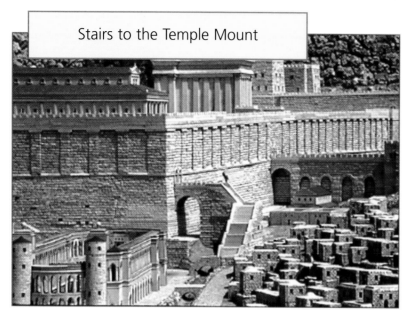

Stairs to the Temple Mount

brother of Joseph, according to Hegesippus) but also through his mother. If this was the case, then Jesus and Simon were first cousins.

Thabuti

But there was another candidate for the position. We have mentioned earlier a certain Thabuti. Just who was this man? The name Thabuti is unique and the name does not seem to have any root in the Hebrew language. Yet Thabuti is mentioned by Josephus and Hegesippus. Several scholars, including A. Hilgenseld, N. Hyldahl, and R. Reisner, suggest that Thabuti was one of the Kohanim (the priests mentioned in Acts 6:7) and that he was an outstanding convert from the Essene community to Christianity. As such, he would have played an important role, and could very well have been of great assistance to James, perhaps even composing the letter attributed to James, as suggested above.

Thabuti is mentioned by Josephus in the following context during the siege of Jerusalem (*Wars of the Jews* 6.8.3):

> In those days, one of the priests came forward, a son of Thabuti, by the name of Jesus, to whom Caesar had promised by oath to save under the condition that he would produce some of the holy treasures. He produced from the wall of the Temple two lamps which were very similar to those in the Temple. Furthermore tables and mixing bowls, all made of gold and well wrought. At the same time, he handed over curtains, the garments of the High Priests that were embroidered with precious stones, and other objects used for the priestly service.

After the time of the destruction of Jerusalem in 70, there were a good number of citizens who had been able to save themselves, and Titus dismissed them wherever they wanted to go. Thabuti apparently was one of these.

Thabuti is also mentioned by Eusebius, citing Hegesippus:

> They used to call the church the virgin since she had not yet been seduced by listening to pointless teaching. But Thabuti, because he had not been

made bishop, began to seduce her. He belonged to one of the seven sects among the people.

Hegesippus names the sects: Essenes, Galileans, Hemerobaptists, Masbotheans, Samaritans, Sadducees, and Pharisees.

That Thabuti had expected to become bishop must have been based on his service to the community. Perhaps he had been an elder in the Essene community. A reason for his aspirations might lie in Essene doctrine, according to which priests had precedence over other members. Even over the Messiah of David. He had accepted James, even though he was not a priest, since he was the brother of the Lord and was such a holy, righteous man. But now that James had given up his life, it was high time that the old system of electing the bishop be reestablished.

We do not know how much time elapsed between the death of James and the election, but it seems they did not follow the usual procedure for elections in the Essene community. When Thabuti realized that a member of the family of David had been selected, he was furious and protested. He had expected to succeed James. He was a priest, an Essene, and may well have been James' right-hand man and, in his own opinion, was the best man qualified for the job.

The protest led to schism. Hegessipus says that Thabuti caused the first rift in the church, which up until then "had been like an untouched virgin" (*Ecclesiastical History* 4.22.4). It may be supposed that Thabuti was the leader of the first heresy in the church (the Ebionites) after the election of Simon Bar Cleophas. His views conflicted with the developing theology of who Jesus was.

It seems that Thabuti was steeped in the basic doctrine of the uniqueness of God, and could not accept the ideas of the preexistence of the Son of God, which became prevalent among the Nazorean clan. He and his followers revolted against the idea of the incarnation of God born of a virgin. For them, Jesus the Son of God meant that he, like Moses, had been adopted to be the Son of God, during the baptism in the Jordan (Adoptionism). Many among the Essenes were threatened by these new ideas and in danger of apostatizing.

The death of James was a cause of great hardships that came upon the community from inside and outside.

Letter to the Hebrews

The Letter to the Hebrews seems to be addressed to priests. Could it have been written for other Essene priests who were in danger of apostasy? We know that priests were still functioning in the Temple, and this must have exerted a certain attraction to the priests of the Essene community on Mount Zion who had accepted Jesus as

Messiah. After the death of James, were they in danger of apostatizing? The great Jewish scholar Yagil Yadin believed that the audience to whom the Letter to the Hebrews was addressed consisted of Essene priests. The same idea was also expressed by H. Kosmala in his book on the connection between Essenes and early Christians.

The Ebionites

The followers of Thabuti kept a name that was prevalent among the Essenes' community of goods, *Ebonim* or "Ebionites," the poor ones. In time they issued a gospel of the Ebionites. The first schism in the church was thus brought about.

Were the infancy narratives of Luke and Matthew a response to Ebionite teaching? The original promising Essene experience unexpectedly took an undesirable direction. R.A. Pritz suggests that the name Nazorean designated those who remained orthodox. And Simon Bar Cleophas, the cousin of Jesus, was the new bishop, which may have increased tensions. The new bishop had doubtless known and loved Jesus as a child. This would have enhanced his position.

Political Revolt

But when Simon took over as leader, he had much to deal with.

Violence was everywhere. In Egypt in 66 there was a revolt of Jews in Alexandria. It was answered quickly by the prefect of Egypt, Tiberius Alexander, who slaughtered thousands of them. Jewish Zealots rioted in Rome in 67, and the outbreak there resulted in many Jews being put to death. Among those who perished were Peter and Paul.

In the summer of 66 Florus had Jews crucified in Jerusalem. And in September of that year, an attack was made by the Syrian governor on Jerusalem. Several of the Christian leaders left the city.

The Jewish-Roman war broke out in earnest after the revolt of the Zealots in 66. The Zealots were a nationalistic group that had come into being at the beginning of the century and became increasingly ferocious and terroristic as the century progressed. Josephus tells us that their numbers and fanaticism increased. They found anything Roman offensive and objected to being governed by a procurator.

The Jewish-Roman War

In Palestine, the Zealot revolt was centered in Caesarea. News of the outbreaks reached Nero in Greece, where he was attending the Olympic Games, and he appointed

Vespasian and his son Titus to restore order in Palestine. Full warfare soon developed. Josephus, one of those sent by the Sanhedrin to defend Galilee, was wounded defending Bethsaida Julius and taken captive.

The Romans soon conquered Galilee and were marching against Jerusalem. It was on this journey that Josephus ingratiated himself with the Romans by foretelling that Vespasian would become emperor. When this came about, he was looked on with favor. The war was interrupted in 69 when Vespasian had to return to Rome as its new emperor. (The deciding vote was cast by Tiberius Alexander, former legate in Egypt, who declared himself for Vespasian, and the whole Orient backed him.) Vespasian's son Titus took over the troops as they marched south, with Tiberius Alexander staunchly supporting him and Josephus taking in all that he saw. Josephus would eventually go back to Rome with Titus to write his history.

Dormition Abbey

The Flight to Pella

In Jerusalem, Simon was able to keep the flock together, but when news reached Jerusalem that Titus was coming close to Jericho and would descend from there to Jerusalem, they thought the time had come to leave the city. In 1981, archaeological excavations carried out by Emmanuel Eisenberg below the annex of the Dormition Abbey discovered a street running in a northerly direction with some poorly built houses flanking both sides. One had a small mikvah. All the buildings were dated to the first century CE and were destroyed in the great conflagration of the year 70. Along the street several coins were found, none of them dating later than 67 or 68. Whoever lived in these houses had abandoned them before the destruction of Jerusalem.

Simon took his Nazoreans and fled with them to Pella in the mountains beyond the Jordan, in the Decapolis.

Eusebius takes up the story:

The members of the Jerusalem church, by means of an oracle given by revelation to acceptable persons there, were ordered to leave the city before the war began, and settle in a town in Perea called Pella. To Pella, those who believed in Christ emigrated from Jerusalem...holy men had utterly abandoned the royal metropolis of the Jews and the entire Jewish land. (*Ecclesiastical History* 3.5.3)

Epiphanius (*Panarion* 29.7.7) also remarks that the flight was undertaken on account of an oracle that might be identified with one in Mark 13:14ff:

But when you see the desolating sacrilege set up where it ought not to be (let the reader understand), then those in Judea must flee to the mountains; the one on the housetop must not go down or enter the house to take anything away; the one in the field must not turn back to get a coat. Woe to those who are pregnant, and to those who are nursing infants in those days! Pray that it may not be in winter. For in those days there will be suffering such as have not been from the beginning of creation. (13:14–19)

The Ebionites apparently decided to remain in the city.

Expectations of the Parousia

Belief in the parousia, the impending coming of Christ, was still strong at this time. Would he return at Pella? Were the Christians moving around in the desert of Gilead in the hope that Jesus might come back? *The Ascension of Isaiah* (an apocryphal Christian writing) says: "And there will be much contention on the eve of His advent and...believers and saints will move from desert to desert in expectation for the return of the 'Beloved One'" (3.22—4.13). This expectation must have been especially strong when they heard that the Holy City and its Temple had been destroyed. But nothing happened. We do not know how the group supported themselves in Pella. Possibly they worked as day laborers.

It was only with the fall of Masada in 73, three years after the destruction of the Temple, that the hope of an early return of Jesus, the parousia, seems to have vanished. Euthycus of Alexandria tells us they (the Nazorean group) returned under the leadership of Simon to Jerusalem "during the fourth year of Vespasian." Upon their return they found the ruins of their former center destroyed with the rest of Jerusalem. But out of the ashes a phoenix would rise. They were ready to start over with a renewed spirit.

CHAPTER FIVE

RETURN TO JERUSALEM
THE YEARS 70–80

At Passover in 70, when pilgrims had poured into Jerusalem from all over the Mediterranean world, the full force of Rome hurled itself against the Jews. Titus laid siege to the city with four legions. Tiberius Alexander, the soldier who had cast the deciding vote to elect Vespasian emperor and second in command, swiftly captured the first wall of the city, then the second and the third, and surrounded the city with a rampart. Resisting Jews were crucified; Josephus reports as many as five hundred a day. He relates: "The soldiers, out of wrath and hatred they bore the Jews, nailed those they caught, one after another, to the crosses by way of jest."

"Famine stalked. Wives robbed their husbands, children their fathers, mothers their babies, snatching the food out of their very mouths."

And he gives an account of a mother killing and eating her baby.

The Antonia Fortress, built by Herod the Great, was captured by the Romans. By the beginning of August, sacrifice in the Temple had ceased. On August 29, the Tenth Legion captured the inner court and set the Temple on fire. Josephus witnessed it all and sat by Titus while he watched it burn. It was the tenth day of the fifth month, the day on which Nebuchadnezzar had set fire to the original Temple of Solomon:

> In the fifth month, on the tenth day of the month, which was the nineteenth year of the King Nebuchadnezzar, King of Babylon, Nebuzaradan, the captain of the bodyguard who served the King of Babylon, entered Jerusalem. He burned the house of the Lord, and the King's house, and all the houses of Jerusalem; every great house he burnt down. (Jer 52:12–13)

This event is still commemorated today as a day of mourning by the Jews, Thesha Deav.

In front of the destroyed Temple, the victorious army offered sacrifices to their own deities.

In September, the upper city was captured and the Herodian palace taken.

One hundred thousand Jews died either from starvation or by the sword. Over ninety thousand others were sent into hard labor in Egypt, or to perish in the circuses with wild beasts. Many Jews were taken to Syria and forced to fight in the gladiator ring. The handsomest and tallest of the youth were kept for the triumphal procession in Rome.

A good number of citizens had been able to save themselves by helping the Romans, and Titus dismissed them wherever they wanted to go. Josephus relates that the son of Thabuti succeeded in paying off General Titus after the capture of Jerusalem with precious gifts he retrieved from a secret hideout:

> Two candlesticks, tables, cisterns, and vials, all made of gold, and very heavy. He also delivered to him the veils and the garments, with the precious stones and a great number of other precious vessels, that belonged to their sacred worship. (*Wars of the Jews* 6.3)

Were these the treasures mentioned in the Copper Scroll? It appears that Thabuti and some Ebionites survived the destruction.

By the end of the year 70, Caesarea was a Roman colony. This meant that the leading inhabitants were given Roman citizenship with all of its benefits. Taxes were remitted and building programs subsidized to ensure loyalty to Rome. Judea was made an imperial province under the rule of the legate of the Tenth Legion in Jerusalem, Lucilius Bassus, who lived in the Herodian palace. The steps leading up to the palace from the Hinnon valley can still be seen today to the south of the Jaffa Gate. (Magen Broshi excavated these in the late 1970s.) The wall to the south of that entry around Mount Zion was completely destroyed, as was the gate of the Essenes and the Essene and Christian quarters.

A detachment of the Tenth Roman Legion occupied the Herodian towers of Phaseal, Hippicus, and Mariamme, which had been ordered preserved by Titus. They erected triumphal columns at the entrance to the Temple mount, signifying the end of Jewish worship in that place.

Josephus describes the degradation of Jerusalem after the war:

> No stranger who had seen the old Judea and the entrancing beautiful suburbs of her capital, and now beheld her present desolation, could have refrained from tears or suppressed a sigh at the greatness of the change. For the war had ruined all the marks of beauty, and no one who knew it of old, coming suddenly upon it, could have recognized the place.

In the summer of 71, the triumph of Titus and Vespasian over Judea was celebrated in Rome with the erection of the great Arch of Titus, which still stands today. The tax formerly subscribed to the Temple by the Jews was now given to the temple of the Roman god, Jupiter.

Masada, Jewish fortress that fell to Rome in 73 CE

The fortress of Machaerus (where John the Baptist was decapitated) and the Herodium (where Herod the Great was buried) were captured in 72.

It would take another year before Masada would fall. In 73, after besieging it for several months, Flavius Silva conquered this fortress. Several hundred Zealots were hiding out at Masada under the leadership of a man called Eleazar. Rather than submit to capture, each man first killed his family, then committed suicide.

After Masada, Flavius Silva was installed as legate of Jerusalem.

Titus returned to Rome and took along Berenice, the sister of Agrippa II, who had become his mistress (she remained with him in Rome until 79 when he became emperor). Josephus also went with him to Rome, where he was set up in a stylish apartment and commissioned to write a history of the Jewish wars. He would eventually write four books, which are invaluable as sources of information about this time.

Rebuilding Their Lives

To those still left in Jerusalem it must have seemed as if the end of the world had come. But the people did not lose hope.

Rabbi Johanan Ben Zakkai, seeing that the Temple was demolished and therefore sacrifice at an end, founded the Academy of Yabneh (Jamnia) as successor to the Sanhedrin. The members of this Jewish group were all Pharisees. Sadducees had disappeared from the scene with the destruction of the Temple. These Jamnian Pharisees gave new form to the expression of Judaism centered solely on the Torah and the synagogue. It was the birth of Rabbinic Judaism.

Return from Pella

When Masada fell, the Christian Jews returned to Jerusalem. According to a tradition laid down later by Eutychius of Alexandria, the people from Pella returned in the fourth year of Vespasian (73 CE). The specific mention of the particular year suggests that the return was not an invention but is based on historical fact. They must by now have realized that the parousia was unlikely to happen soon and made the decision to return to Jerusalem.

Hegessipus tells us of a situation that must have been a cause for concern among them: "After the capture of Jerusalem, Vespasian issued an order to ensure that no member of the royal house would be left among the Jews. All descendants of David were to be ferreted out. This resulted in a further dispersion of the Jews." We do not know whether any members of the Mount Zion community were in Jerusalem when this order was handed down.

Eusebius refers to the group of returnees as "a very large church of Jews in Jerusalem." The Essene quarter and the Cenacle building lay in ruins, as did most of Jerusalem. "Wild foxes were living among the ruins of the Temple," a later writer tells us. But the group took courage and rebuilt their center on the spot where the ancient Cenacle, the upper room, had stood. It became their synagogue. Judaism was still a *religio licita*, a religion permitted by the Romans, so they were allowed to build a prayer center. They referred to their house of worship as a synagogue and would continue to do so for several centuries. Even some gentile Christian groups called their houses synagogues, as we see from Ignatius of Antioch's letter *To Polycarp* and from Justin Martyr's *Dialogue with Tryphon*.

In 1951, archaeologist Joseph Pinkerfield found on Mount Zion the remains of a synagogue and concluded that the building had been constructed after 70 CE. But unlike other synagogues, the synagogue did not face the destroyed Temple but instead faced the place of the resurrection. Pinkerfield also found pieces of plaster with graffiti scratched on them that came from the synagogue wall. A team of experts from the Studium Biblicum Franciscanum, led by Professors Emmanuel Testa and Bellarmino Bagatti, published the graffiti. Their interpretation is as follows: "One graffito has the initials of the Greek words which may be translated as 'conquer, savior, mercy.' Another graffito has the letters which can be translated as 'O Jesus, that I may live, O Lord of the autocrat.'"

Archaeologists believe that the large and beautiful ashlars used in the construction of this synagogue are stones that came from a Herodian building. Since the upper palace remained standing for the Tenth Legion, it is most likely that the stones used came from the Temple area. In size and shape they are similar to the stones lying north of the Robinson arch today. These stones were put to secondary use in the new synagogue of the Jewish Christians. They are still visible today underneath the Cenacle.

Carrying stones from the Temple to establish a new synagogue had precedent. The Talmud records that exiles from Jerusalem to Babylon had brought stones from Jerusalem that they incorporated into a synagogue as a substitute for the Temple. The cornerstone of the synagogue at Djerba in Tunisia is believed to have been taken from the Temple of Solomon in the fifth century BCE. This can still be seen today.

The New Zion

The community also transferred the idea of Zion from the Temple to their own place, the Neo Sion. The old Zion was destroyed. They were convinced, as was Josephus Flavius, that the original city of David had been located at the site of their new synagogue. But the archaeological evidence does not support them in this belief. The fortress conquered by David was above the Gihon fountain on the Ophel.

They may have been wrong, but they were happy in this thought of David's city, since Simon Bar Cleophas, their leader, was from the house of David. In later years, the author of the *Odes of Solomon* complained that they had no right to change the name of the old place to a new one since God himself had chosen this:

> No man can pervert your holy place, O my God
> Nor can he change it and put it in another place
> Because he has not the power over it;
> For your sanctuary you designed before you made special places.

The returned Jewish Christians were pleased with their new building. It carries the honor of being called the "Mother of all churches" (Mater Panton Ekklesion). In 381 the Jewish Christians on Mount Zion were reconciled with the Grand Byzantine church, and under Emperor Theodosius an octagonal portico was added to the original building and was called the Church of the Apostles. At that time a pillar, thought to have been the pillar of the flagellation, was brought from the ruins of the house of the high priest, Caiaphas, and incorporated into it. The pillar and column are mentioned both by Egeria and by Paula, women pilgrims of the fourth century.

In the fifth century, Bishop John II of Jerusalem built on the site a magnificent basilica that had eighty pillars. It commemorated the place where Mary lived after the resurrection, and where she died. This church was destroyed by Hakim the Sultan of Egypt in 1009. In the twelfth century the Crusaders incorporated the ruins of that sanctuary into their church of Sancta Maria in Mount Zion and built the present upper room (Cenacle). Pope John Paul II, during his pilgrimage to Israel in 2000 CE, was the first priest in five centuries to offer Mass at the place where it was instituted.

Worship and Liturgy

The Jewish Christians met regularly in the synagogue. The primary purpose of the synagogue was not for prayer but for the reading, studying, and expounding of scripture.

Synagogues catered to various congregations, such as fellow countrymen, craftsmen guilds, freed slaves, and so on. A head of the synagogue was elected but we do not know how he was chosen. He had to be an educated man who was familiar with rites and could judge the competence of those called to read Scripture. The synagogue was run by the community. If a priest happened to be there he was just one of the congregation. Ten adult males needed to be present for the service, which was very long, beginning before sunrise and ending in time for the midday meal. There were blessings both before and after the readings. The person who led the prayers was not appointed to do so permanently; he was a member who was asked to come forward and read. He read from the Torah and the Prophets and someone stood beside him and translated from the Hebrew so that all could understand. Any member was then invited to comment on what had been read.

Synagogue attendance was confined to Sabbath (Saturday) and to feast days. Often there was a school attached to the synagogue, since numerous Jewish laws called for the education of children. We can only surmise that the Christian synagogue community in Jerusalem had its own school, and at its Sabbath services interpreted the Scriptures in the light of the life and resurrection of Christ.

Synagogue wall under Cenacle

Home Churches

For the Jews, dining in community was an important institution. On many occasions the dinners were held in the homes of one of the members of the synagogue. The Jewish-Christian community celebrated the Eucharist in homes on Sunday, a ceremony reserved for baptized Christians. The prayers and reading doubtless followed the model of the synagogue readings for the Sabbath. The

Didache relates that the Lord's Prayer was also used complete with the doxology, and it preserves the prayer for the consecration of the cup: "We give thanks to thee, our Father, for the Holy vine of David thy child which thou didst make known to us through Jesus thy servant. To thee be glory forever."

One of the oldest eucharistic prayers we have is ascribed to James, "the brother of the Lord." Scholars agree that it is very ancient.

And when he was about to endure his voluntary death on the cross, the sinless for us sinners, on the night when he was betrayed (or rather handed himself over) for the life and salvation of the world, he took bread in his holy, undefiled, blameless, and immortal hands, looked up to heaven and showed it to you, his God and Father; he gave thanks, blessed, sanctified and broke it and gave it to his holy and blessed disciples and apostles saying "Take, eat, this is my body, which is broken and distributed for you for forgiveness of sins." Likewise after supper he took the cup, he mixed wine and water, he looked up to heaven and showed it to you his God and Father; he gave thanks, blessed and sanctified it, filled it with the Holy Spirit and gave it to his holy and blessed disciples and apostles, saying "Drink from it, all of you; this is my blood of the new covenant which is shed and distributed for you and for many for the forgiveness of sins. Do this for my remembrance"; for as often as you eat this bread and drink this cup, you proclaim the death of the Son of Man and confess his Resurrection, until he comes.

(This version, according to R.C.D. Jasper and G.J. Cuming, is a result of a fusion between the old Jerusalem rite with the anaphora of Saint Basil. It is discussed extensively by A. Tarby, who believes it to have come from Jerusalem, in "La Prière Eucharistique de L'église de Jérusalem.")

We know from the *Didache* that prayer was urged three times a day, which was a custom with the Essenes but not with other groups. The Mishnah says that the Shema should be recited twice a day by individuals, in the morning and in the evening. In Jerusalem, Monday and Thursday were market days when those from the country districts gathered in the towns. In some devout circles it was a time for fasting. Christians, however, observed different days. The *Didache* warns against fasting "with the hypocrites" and says that it should be done on Wednesday and Friday.

Baptism was the formal means of entry into the church. The service would have required "living water," which may have come from the Gihon Spring or the Essene Mikvah. The candidate, who had undergone a fast, went down into the pool as if to death and then rose again to new life.

Celebration of Holy Week

Holy Week was celebrated according to the Essene calendar, on which Passover always fell on Wednesday. In contrast to this practice, which was based on the Synoptic Gospels, was the Johannine tradition, which followed the practice of the Jerusalem Pharisees. (In John's Gospel, Jesus died on the eve of Passover while the lambs were slaughtered in the Temple. This idea was essential to the symbol that Jesus was the Lamb of God, slaughtered on the fifteenth of Nisan.) This brought about a liturgical difference between the East and the West and the very obnoxious quarrel about the celebration of Easter. On one side were the churches of Jerusalem, Rome, and Alexandria, and on the other the places that followed the practice of the Pharisees in the churches in Asia Minor. That quarrel between the Eastern and Western churches was only finally solved by the decision of Nicea in 325.

The Citadel, which protected Jerusalem for many centuries because of its location high on a hill

Writings

The years between 70 and 80 saw the writing of both Luke's and Matthew's Gospels. Eyewitnesses were dying. The accounts, if they were to last, needed to be committed to paper.

Mark's Gospel is usually dated at 70 CE and Luke's at 85 CE. Luke must have come to Jerusalem about the year 75 to get the information that he needed. He says in the introduction to his Gospel that he interviewed eyewitnesses:

Since many have undertaken to set down an orderly account of the events that have been fulfilled among us, just as they were handed on to us by those who from the beginning were eyewitnesses and servants of the word, I too decided, after investigating everything carefully from the very first, to write an orderly account for you, most excellent Theophilus, so that you may know the truth concerning the things about which you have been instructed. (Luke 1:1–5)

Jerusalem was not new to him. He had been there before with Paul. From Antioch he would take a boat from the port of Daphne to Ptolemais, then on to Caesarea, and then travel through Antipatris to Jerusalem. He seems to have had a very good knowledge of Jerusalem and the way to Caesarea: "When we had finished the voyage from Tyre, we arrived at Ptolemais…the next day we left and came to Caesarea…we got ready and started to go up to Jerusalem" (Acts 21:7ff).

He had a personal knowledge of this area of the country, having traveled there with Paul, which stands in contrast to his apparent lack of knowledge of the geography of the north of the country, especially Galilee, as is evident from his Gospel.

Scholars through the years have pointed out that in writing his Gospel, Luke had access to the Gospel of Mark, the collection of sayings designated Q, and his own source that is not shared by other gospel writers. Some scholars (R. Heard, B. Streeter, V. Taylor) are of the opinion that there existed a written Palestinian source from which he drew.

In Jerusalem, Luke certainly would have consorted with the community under Simon Bar Cleophas. Did this community possess a written document with stories of Jesus, composed by a member of the family of the Lord? Among the stories were there the memories of events that had been related by Mary? "She kept these words in her heart." Was Luke given access to the stories from which he made his own composition?

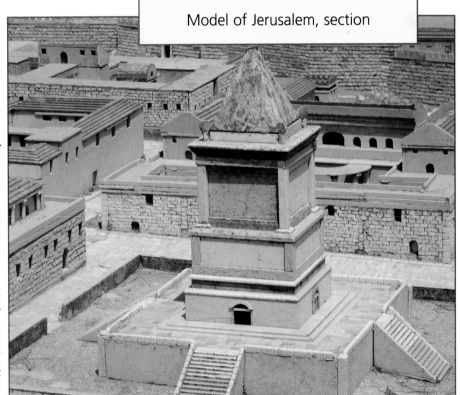

Model of Jerusalem, section

Were the hymns that we find in Luke—the Benedictus, the Nunc Dimittis, and the Magnificat—hymns used by the community? We find all sorts of accounts of angels, which shows an Essene influence, as do the series of commentaries and the stress on the Davidic descent. To the original stories Luke added a few touches of his own.

One story, found only in Luke, could have been related by Simon Bar Cleophas himself. It is the road to Emmaus story: "Now on that same day, two of them were going to a village called Emmaus…Jesus himself came near and went with them…one of them whose name was Cleopas, answered him…" (Luke 24:13ff).

Was the companion of Cleophas his son Simon, now bishop of Jerusalem? When the two disciples returned to Jerusalem, they found the Eleven gathered together and those who were with them, and heard the words "the Lord has risen indeed and he has appeared to Simon" (Luke 24:34). Could this Simon possibly have meant Simon Bar Cleophas? Luke mentions that only the women had seen him that morning and that their testimony was not believed. He writes that the apostles were startled and frightened, and that later that day when Jesus appeared among them, they thought they were seeing a ghost.

Luke doubtless met up with women in Jerusalem, some of whom may well have been witnesses to the resurrection. Quite unusually, he gives the names of certain women: Mary called Magdalene, Joanna, Susanna. These women who had accompanied Jesus from Galilee may have been a source of information about the relationship of Jesus to women. His Gospel is often referred to as the Gospel of women. It avoids anything derogatory about women. He omits the story of the daughter of Herodias asking for the head of John the Baptist, and he does not make mention of either the Samaritan woman at the well who had had five husbands or the woman taken in adultery. Women are present at the birth of Jesus, at his death, and all times in between. They are the bearers of joy. He presents a Jesus who sympathizes with the tasks they perform: the caring for children, sewing of patches, sweeping of houses, bread baking, searching for lost coins, grinding grain, lighting the lamps, and providing food. The important teachings of Jesus on the kingdom, prayer, God, and love involve stories of women. This strongly suggests that women were a source for Luke, and perhaps they were among those he met in the Christian community in Jerusalem.

Matthew

The region of Syria was possibly, according to the *Jerome Biblical Commentary*, the place of writings of Matthew's Gospel. There were many Jewish Christians there, especially around the Batanea, Coelosyria, and Perea. They had fled from Jerusalem and settled down there before the fall of Jerusalem.

Scholars agree that Matthew shared two sources in common with Luke: Mark's Gospel and the Q source. He also had his own particular source of information.

Was Matthew's source for the infancy stories another branch of Jesus' family connected with Joseph? Julius Africanus tells that they lived at Kochaba in the Batanea close to Syria.

Being able to trace ancestry was important. We know that centuries earlier, on returning from the Babylonian Captivity, several were excluded from the priestly class because they could not prove their Levitical pedigree (I Esd 2:62; II Esd 7:64); the prophecy that the Messiah was to be born of the tribe of Judah and the house of David rendered the genealogy important. Eusebius quotes Julius Africanus' letter to Aristides on the harmony of the gospel genealogies: "The disponia (family) kept genealogies based on the official report and made them up as well as they could," suggesting that they were not always entirely accurate.

Both evangelists seem to have had completely different sources for the infancy narrative. But they agree on certain things: the virginal conception and the birth in Bethlehem. There must have been a basic family tradition about Bethlehem and the virgin birth, a tradition that Mark and Paul did not know.

But why so much emphasis on the virgin birth? Was this an argument against the Ebionites, who believed that Jesus was the product of the union of Mary and Joseph and had become God's son only at the time of his baptism? Raymond Brown would seem to agree with this. In his definitive book *The Birth of the Messiah,* he says that opposition to the virginal conception came from those who were denying the divinity of Jesus.

> In church history among the earliest opponents of the virginal conception were those who denied the humanity of Jesus. There were groups that denied the virginal conception. Christian Gnostics, who did so, were often influenced by doctrinal prejudices of a domestic or anti-worldly nature. Not the manner of the conception but the fact of conception (taking flesh in the womb) was repugnant to them. Most important for our purpose was the rejection of the virginal conception by some Jewish Christians who accepted Jesus as the Messiah of strictly human origin. The roots of these groups in Palestine raise the possibility, albeit slight, of a tradition of natural conception coming down in Palestine from the original Jews who believed in Jesus.

Eusebius tells us that the Ebionites started the first schism in the community on this issue. Were the infancy narratives of both Luke and Matthew written to contradict them? Was the story of the annunciation meant to counteract that opinion?

Neither Luke's nor Matthew's Gospel would be available until the year 85. It was Matthew's Gospel that then became popular with the Nazorean Christians. This can be explained in that while Luke's Gospel was addressed to the gentiles, Matthew's was addressed to the Jews. And the group in Jerusalem was Jewish.

CHAPTER SIX

WRITINGS, LITURGY, HIERARCHY THE YEARS 80–100

Attempts to promote the Imperial cult had been made in Israel under Herod the Great and his sons. Excavations at Caesarea Maritima and at Omrit show temples dedicated to Augustus that had been built by Herod the Great. At Bethsaida, his son, Philip Herod, had built a small temple to the wife of Augustus, Livia Julia. The Herod family had demonstrated its loyalty to Rome by such displays. But such temples were anathema to the Jews, and Jews themselves were exonerated from observance of the Imperial cult. Successive Roman emperors after Augustus had been hailed "divine Lord." Most had shunned this appellation. But there were those like Gaius and Nero who gloried in it, as did Domitian, who became emperor in 81.

Domitian was an appallingly cruel man who took the appellation "divine" seriously. All government procla-mations began "Our lord and God Domitian." Those who refused to take an oath to him were exiled, imprisoned, or put to death. (John, the author of the Book of Revelation, was sentenced to confinement on the island of Patmos during the reign of Domitian.) Great numbers of distinguished men in Rome were put to death without trial, and others were exiled and their property confiscated. Domitian had his cousin Flavius Clemens condemned to death as a Christian.

Herod's palace at Masada

Persecution of Christians by the Romans had been confined to Rome until this period, but now it was extended all over the Empire. Governors who wished to curry favor with the emperor, and there were plenty of them in the provinces, promoted the cult of the emperor and insisted on oaths of loyalty to the Lord God Domitian. Jews and Christians could not in conscience take this oath. These were dangerous times.

The capital of the Imperial cult was Ephesus. The Book of Revelation, an apocalyptic piece of literature, was written at this time as a response to the persecutions in Ephesus and the surrounding cities.

In Jerusalem, a shrine of Jupiter was erected on the temple grounds. Prayers for the emperor were said daily in the Temple and this had been accepted. But a memorial to the chief Roman god must have caused some consternation among devout Jews.

At the same time, Hegessipus tells us that Domitian ordered the execution of all descendants of David. Eusebius gives Hegessipus' account of what happened to Jude's grandsons:

> The grandsons of Jude, who was said to be His [Jesus'] brother, humanly speaking, were informed against as being of David's line, and brought by the evocatus before Domitian Caesar, who was as afraid of the advent of Christ as Herod had been. Domitian asked them whether they were descended from David and they admitted it. Then he asked them what property they owned and what funds they had at their disposal. They replied that they had only 9,000 denarii between them, half belonging to each; this they said, was not available in cash, but was the estimated value of only twenty five acres of land, from which they raised the money to pay their taxes and the wherewithal to support themselves by their toil.

Then, the writer tells us, they showed him their hands, putting forward as proof of their toil the hardness of their bodies and the calluses impressed on their hands by incessant labor. When asked about Christ and his kingdom, what it was like, and where and when it would appear, they explained that it was not of this world or anywhere on earth but angelic and in heaven, and would be established at the end of the world, when he would come in glory to judge the living and the dead and give every person payment according to his or her conduct. On hearing this, "Domitian found no fault with them but despising them, as beneath his notice, let them go free and issued orders terminating the persecution of the Church." Eusebius hastens to add that this applied to the Jerusalem church only.

Another ancient summary says: "When Domitian spoke with the sons of Jude, the brother of the Lord, and learned of the virtue of the men, he brought to an end the persecution against us." This report gives their names as Zoker and James.

Epiphanius stresses that Domitian was impressed by their "wisdom." What clever men they were! As they were being tried for their lives, they gave an argument that the money they had went first of all to pay taxes! Eusebius tell us that the sons of Jude eventually became leaders of the Jewish Christians in their communities in Galilee.

Remains of temple to Livia Julia (wife of Augustus), built by Philip Herod in 30 CE

Domitian was assassinated by order of his wife in 96. Those who were banished returned. The Roman Senate elected one of their own number, Nerva, to replace him. Two years later Nerva's adopted son, Trajan, an army general, became emperor.

Jerusalem

After the destruction of the Temple, the Pharisees had moved to Jamnia, a small town just south of modern Tel Aviv where new life was being given to Judaism in the context of the synagogue. The Nazoreans (who had returned from Pella) and the Ebionites were left in Jerusalem, as were fringe groups of Gnostics. (Exclusion of heretics only occurred after the year 150. They were merely considered as people who had different opinions.) Epiphanius in the *Panarion* says that Essenes had mostly moved to the other side of the Jordan and many became Ebionites.

Simon Bar Cleophas continued as episcopus over his flock. He was the one living link with Jesus, having actually known him. It is said that God preserved Simon so long in the church so that the true tradition could be transmitted. Assisted by a group of elders, he dealt with the many concerns as they arose.

The community continued to meet in their synagogue on Saturdays and in their homes for the Eucharist on Sundays.

What Was Being Written?

While oral tradition was the main way of transmission in the early years, much was also written down. This was the time when a hypothetical gospel of the deeds of Jesus, "the signs gospel," may have been written (according to Peter Kirkby and Robert Fortna). This document would have mentioned many places, such as the pool of Bethesda and its five porticos, the Lithostrotos, and Bethany, which indicates that its provenance was Jerusalem. The writer would certainly have been familiar with the geography of Judea. This "signs" precanonical gospel, as it is being called, may have been put together by an early community of Jewish followers of Jesus in what one scholar calls "the full flush of enthusiasm about their recently departed Messiah." The sayings of Jesus, a collection of logia (the Q source), were also preserved and transmitted, although whether Q was oral or written is an open question. Since it was a source used by both Luke and Matthew it may well have been written down.

Steps heading up to Herodian palace

By the early eighties, many other documents were being written. Luke, whose Gospel is usually dated at 85, reminds us that "many have undertaken to complete a narrative of the things that have been accomplished among us."

Copies of the letters of Paul were in circulation, possibly soon after his death. They are mentioned in the letter of Clement of Rome in 95.

The *Didache*

The *Didache*, a short book only rediscovered in 1873 by the Orthodox Metropolitan of Constantinople, claims to be instructions, given to the apostles based on the sayings of Jesus, for those who wished to become Christian. Baptism was to be conferred in "the name of the Father, and of the son, and of the Holy Ghost" in living water. The person to be baptized, and if possible the baptizer, had to fast for one or two days beforehand. If the water was insufficient for immersion it had to be poured three times on the head. As mentioned earlier, it tells that fasts were not to be on Mondays and Thursdays as the Jews fasted, but on Tuesdays and Fridays. Christians must not pray with the "hypocrites," but must say the Our Father. It contains short extracts of the Sermon on the Mount and gives rules for behavior, such as which vices to avoid (one vice leads to another, anger to murder, concupiscence to adultery).

> Concerning the Eucharist, thus you shall give thanks: We give you thanks our Father, for the holy vine of David, thy child, which thou hast made known to us through Jesus thy child; to thee be glory forever. For as this broken bread was dispersed over the mountains, and being collected became one, so may thy church be gathered together from the ends of the earth into thy Kingdom, for thine is the glory and the power forever through Jesus Christ. And let none eat or drink of your Eucharist except those who have been baptized in the name of Christ; for of this the Lord said "give not holy things to dogs."

The book gives a thanksgiving after communion in which mention is made of the "spiritual food and drink and eternal life through thy child."

The words in thanksgiving for the chalice are: "It is he who has poured out the wine, the blood of the vine of David, upon our wounded souls." The chalice is mentioned before the bread, which is in accordance with the Jewish blessing of wine and bread, and with Luke 22:17–19. (The Essenes blessed the bread before the wine.)

This book speaks of teachers and prophets. Every apostle is to be received "as the Lord, and he may stay for one or two days, but if he stays for three days, he is a false prophet." If he asks for money he is a false prophet. Prophets are known by their morals.

The breaking of bread and thanksgiving is on Sundays, "after you have confessed your transgression so that your sacrifice may be pure." The instruction continues: "Ordain for yourselves bishops and deacons...for they minister to you the ministries of prophets and teachers." It does not mention presbyters. We know that there were presbyters by the time of the writing of the letter of Clement of Rome to the Corinthian community in the year 95.

The last chapter exhorts the faithful to be watchful, and tells the signs of the end of the world.

Scholars point out the similarity to the later Jewish Talmud. Jewish influence was still strong. Interestingly it states: "Do not start a schism but pacify contending parties." Could this refer to the Ebionite sect?

Most scholars now agree that the *Didache* was produced prior to the end of the century, and that its provenance was Jerusalem.

The Letter of Jude

Was the letter of Jude written at this time? Recent scholarship has placed the letter between 80 and 100, and its provenance as Jerusalem. Was it written by "the brother of James," as he claims? Jude would have been a very old man by that time and this letter reflects no lack of mental acuteness. It is probably pseudonymous, written by an author who wanted to connect himself to the family of Jesus, or perhaps even by a member of that family through Jude. The sons of Jude lived on into the reign of Trajan. The primary intent of the letter is to defend orthodox Christianity. Jude urges the readers to fight hard for the faith delivered once for all to the saints.

The Odes of Solomon

The Odes of Solomon consist of forty-two hymns of praise and ethical exhortations. They have been referred to as the first Christian hymnbook. They were written in the type of Hebrew used at Qumran, and scholars have noted the striking parallels between the *Odes* and the Dead Sea Scrolls: Both have a consciousness of "the way," the term used by Paul to describe the early followers of Christ. There is emphasis on "knowledge," "war," "crown," and "living waters"; the gentiles are shown in unattractive terms; there is stress on baptism. The author may have been influenced by the philosophy appearing in the Dead Sea Scrolls, or, as James Charlesworth suggests, the author may have been at one time a member of the Essenes. The *Odes* are dated by Charlesworth before the year 100. They are Christian documents and show a belief in the incarnation:

> He has generously shown himself to me
> Because his kindness has diminished his grandeur
> He became like me, that I might receive him.
> In form he was considered like me,
> That I might put him on.
> And I trembled when I saw him
> Because he was gracious to me.
> Like my nature he became
> That I might understand him.
> and the crucifixion:
> I extended my hands
> And hallowed my Lord;
> For the expansion of my hands
> Is the upright cross.
> …

I extended my hands and approached my Lord,
Because the stretching out of my hands is his sign
And my extension is the common cross
That was lifted up on the way of the Righteous One.
and the resurrection:
Then I rose and am with them
And will speak by their mouths.
Like the arm of the bridegroom over the bride,
So is my yoke over those who know me.
I was not rejected although I was considered to be so,
And I did not perish although they thought it of me.

Gentiles Now Dominant

By the last two decades of the first century, Christianity had spread widely. Gentiles by now far outnumbered Jews in the church worldwide. There were major centers of Christianity at Antioch, Alexandria, Ephesus, and Rome, as well as at Jerusalem. All of these except for Jerusalem were gentile communities. Each community operated according to its own rules and many different practices were tolerated. This was the case until the Council of Nicea in 325.

The churches organized themselves and developed systems of authority. The pastoral letters and the first letter of Peter address bishops, deacons, and elders. Qualifications for these men (and women in the case of deacons) were stringent, as we learn from these letters:

Whoever aspires to the office of bishop desires a noble task. Now a bishop must be above reproach, married only once, temperate, sensible, responsible, hospitable, and an apt teacher, not a drunkard, not violent but gentle, not quarrelsome and not a lover of money. (1 Tim 3:1–5)

Deacons likewise must be serious, not double-

Seal of Solomon on the ancient synagogue at Capernaum

tongued, not indulging in much wine, not greedy for money; they must hold fast to the mystery of the faith with a clear conscience. And let them first be tested; then, if they prove themselves blameless, let them serve as deacons. Women likewise must be serious, not slanderers, but temperate, faithful in all things. Let deacons be married only once, and let them manage their children and their households well; for those who serve well as deacons gain a good standing for themselves and great boldness in the faith that is in Christ Jesus. (1 Tim 3:8–13)

I left you behind in Crete for this reason, that you should put in order what remained to be done, and should appoint elders in every town, as I directed you: someone who is blameless, married only once, whose children are believers, not accused of debauchery and not rebellious. For a bishop, as God's steward, must be blameless; he must not be arrogant or quick-tempered or addicted to wine or violent or greedy for gain; but he must be hospitable, a lover of goodness, prudent, upright, devout, and self-controlled. He must have a firm grasp of the word that is trustworthy in accordance with the teaching, so that he may be able both to preach with sound doctrine and to refute those who contradict it. (Titus 1:5–10)

Now as an elder myself and a witness of the sufferings of Christ, as well as one who shares in the glory to be revealed, I exhort the elders among you to tend the flock of God that is in your charge, exercising the oversight, not under compulsion but willingly, as God would have you do it—not for sordid gain but eagerly. Do not lord it over those in your charge, but be examples to the flock. And when the chief shepherd appears, you will win the crown of glory that never fades away. (1 Pet 5:1–4)

But there was no one formula. The question of final authority still was not settled. The letter of Clement of Rome directs that all questions should be referred to the bishop. The letter of Ignatius of Antioch (106) warns his congregation to be obedient to the bishop. This followed the practice of the Essenes who were submissive in all things to their overseer *(megaqqer)*. Bishops were elected and collegially responsible for service for all. Did the idea of bishop *(megaqqer)* originate in the Jerusalem community?

Jerusalem was still heeded in its practices. For the whole church the practice of fast days in Jerusalem was decisive. Fast was on Wednesday and Friday because Jesus was taken prisoner and killed on those days. For other Jews, the fast days were Monday and Thursday.

Eventually all the churches came to adopt one bishop as the overseer in each community. By the end of the century, the position of presybters replaced the elders and they presided over the celebration of the Eucharist.

Day-to-day Existence

From the *Letter of Hermes* we know that the community ministered to widows and orphans and the destitute, and that they were hospitable, reverenced the aged, were gentle, practiced justice, and did not oppress the poor debtor. Simon as bishop, along with his other duties, would have been in charge of dispensing hospitality and sheltering the destitute and widows. The *Didache* directs that there were to be no idle Christians (as indeed does the letter of James). Moving forward with the message of Jesus, the passing on of the tradition of the life, ministry, and passion of Jesus, and the establishment of sound doctrine were the main focuses of the Jewish community in these years.

While we know that there were persecutions in other parts of the Empire (particularly around Ephesus), we do not know how prevalent persecution of the Jewish Christians in Jerusalem was at this time. Were they regarded as Jews or as something different? Doubtless the decree against the members of the house of David must have kept the community on guard. This decree would eventually lead to the execution of Simon Bar Cleophas.

CHAPTER SEVEN

REBELLIONS, PERSECUTION, AND DIVISION: THE YEARS 100–135

The first three decades of the second century would bring many changes. At the beginning of the new century, Trajan was emperor of Rome. He is reputed to have been a capable and just ruler, occupied with expanding the Empire, building roads and harbors, erecting public buildings in Rome, and maintaining order within his vast territories. But there were revolts all over the Empire.

In Palestine, a Roman colony was established at Schechem and named Flavia Neapolis. Vespasian had settled eight hundred veterans in Emmaus after the war and had given them land. Pagan encroachment was increasing in Israel. Claudius Atticus Herodius was appointed procurator of Judea and resided in the Herodian palace at Caesarea. He commanded the Roman forces, the Tenth Legion, who were stationed in and around Jerusalem. The city was still largely in rubble since the 70s' war. Remnants of the old population who still lived in the city had to pay the Temple tax to the *fiscus Judaicus* for the support of the Roman god Jupiter Capitolinus, whose statue stood on the Temple ground. Jewish Christians must have been subject to this tax.

The supreme council of Judaism had moved to Jamnia. *Religio licita*, which gave protection of religion to established religions, was still in effect. Jewish literature

Beth Shean, head city of the Decapolis

from this period gives no indication of a split between the Nazoreans and the Jews. The Jewish-Christian group in Jerusalem was thus protected under this Roman regulation. We know that Christians, both Jewish and gentile, were being persecuted in other parts of the Empire.

But for many Jews, the hope of the restoration of Israel under an expected Messiah remained alive. In their long history, Jerusalem had been conquered before, and the Temple had been destroyed and rebuilt. God had not abandoned them. The scriptures contained promises of God's ultimate intervention on their behalf.

Resentment against Roman rule fermented and was felt especially in the Diaspora. Rabbinic literature makes reference to various revolts throughout the Empire, as does Dio Cassius, a Roman historian of the second century. Josephus, who wrote so eloquently about the Jewish wars, had died in the year 100.

In 107 a revolt broke out in Jerusalem that resulted in the death of Simon Bar Cleophas. The instruction of Domitian that ordered the execution of all descendants of David did not seem to have been revoked.

Eusebius writes:

> Some of these heretics charged Simon, son of Cleophas, with being a descendant of David and a Christian; as a result he suffered martyrdom at the age of 120, when Trajan was Emperor and Atticus consular governor.

It is unlikely that Simon was 120. Eusebius doubtless was stressing that Simon was a very old man. (The author of Genesis 5 claims that Methuselah lived for 969 years!)

Sadly, not only the political authorities were now to be dreaded, but also traitors within the family itself. Simon was the last of the eyewitnesses. With him would end the period of those who had known Jesus.

Hegesippus gives us the story:

> The son of the Lord's uncle, the aforesaid Simon Bar Cleophas, was similarly informed against by the heretical sects and brought up on the same charge before Atticus, the provincial governor. Tortured for days on end, he bore a martyr's witness, so that all, including the governor, were astounded that at the age of 120 he could endure it; and he was ordered to be crucified.

In his forty-five-year reign, Simon's steady hand had guided his community through a most difficult stage in its history. His election after the horribly violent death of James had been met with divisiveness. The first heresy of the Ebionites, had, as Eusebius says, destroyed the virginity of the church. He had received the news of the martyrdom of the apostles in Rome and found himself among the few who were still witnesses to the resurrection.

Hegesippus tells of the end of the age of innocence:

> The generation of those privileged to listen with their own ears to the divine wisdom had passed on, then godless error began to take shape, through the deceit of false teachers, who, now that none of the apostles were left, threw off the mask and attempted to counter the preaching of the truth by preaching the knowledge (gnosis) falsely so called.

Simon had seen the threat posed by the Zealot revolt in 66 and taken his group to the safety of Pella. Here he had held them together through their disappointment in the parousia. He had supervised their reestablishment in Jerusalem and the building of their synagogue on Mount Zion, encouraged the establishment of the new liturgies, and kept contact with their Jewish roots. Through the turbulent eighties he had held on to the message of the apostles despite innovations that were tending to draw off sizable portions of his flock. He had encouraged his congregation not to lose heart through persecutions. And now at a very advanced age he was betrayed by members of his own community.

It is poignant that Simon was betrayed by one of his own, just as his cousin, Jesus, had been handed over by his friend. The Romans crucified Simon even though he was at an advanced age. Was subjecting him to such a humiliating death meant to set an example to his followers? The Romans had little sympathy for age.

Like Judas, the informers did not benefit by their treachery. We do not know who they were, but Eusebius said that they themselves were later executed.

After the turmoil that surely must have followed, a new successor was chosen. The place of Simon was taken by Justus (*Tzadik*), who was also of the family, a descendant of David. Justus must also have known the dangers that faced him in taking over the leadership.

Descendants of David

Being a descendant of David continued to be all-important to the Nazoreans. The ancient prophecies had predicted that the Messiah would be a descendant of David. Herod the Great had tried to falsify his own genealogy to make himself so. Bar Kokhba, who would lead the great rebellion of 135, would make a similar claim.

Bishops of Jerusalem

According to Eusebius, there were thirteen bishops of Jerusalem between the death of Simon and the rebellion of 135. If this was the case, and if indeed they succeeded one another, the average length of service was a little more than two years, which makes one suspect that many met violent deaths. And in Palestine that meant crucifixion.

Eusebius gives the names of the bishops of Jerusalem in that twenty-eight-year period: Zacchaeus followed Justus, then Tobias, Benjamin, John, Matthias, Philip, Seneca, Justus II, Levi, Ephres, Joseph, and Judas. Eusebius makes it clear that his source is Hegesippus, who may have known some of them. Epiphanius of Salamis gives a list of twenty-seven, of which the first fifteen correspond to those of Eusebius. But whether they were all bishops has been argued by scholars. Adolf von Harnack suggests that some were just presbyters (collegia). Gunther Van de Brock notes that the latter six names occur in the apocryphal letter of James to Quadratus. They are described by Bauckham as "respected scribes of the Jews" who had converted to Christianity and who may have been co-workers with James. Bauckham suggests that James had set up a college of twelve to rule with him.

Eusebius writes: "I have not found many written statements of the dates of the bishops of Jerusalem, for tradition says that they were extremely short-lived."

MARTYRDOM

The attitude toward martyrdom was that in embracing it one was imitating the passion of Christ. As such it was to be sought after rather then shunned.

Ignatius of Antioch, already an old man, met his death in 107. He made the journey from Antioch to Rome under strict military guard but along the way was allowed to make speeches and to write letters. Heresies were then creeping into the church and this was a cause of concern to Ignatius, who wrote to the people of Smyrna, Ephesus, and Rome to preserve the message passed on to them by the apostles. Ignatius did not shrink from martyrdom. In fact, he seemed to welcome it. "Wild animals are ready for me. I pray that I may find them prompt. I shall coax them to devour me promptly. If they are unwilling...I will compel them to do it." In the letter he sent to Polycarp of Smyrna he adds a note: "I know and am convinced that even after the Resurrection He was in the flesh. When he came to Peter and his companions, He said to them: 'Take hold, handle me, and see that I am not a bodiless phantom' and they at once touched him and were convinced." Gnosticism was well developed and doubtless his last remark was directed against them. They were producing books that "were spurious and foreign to apostolic orthodoxy" (Eusebius). Ignatius scorned all attempts to rescue him.

Claimants to Be the Messiah

Between 100 and 135 many men (some of whom were deranged) claimed to be the messiah. When the revolutionary Bar Kokhba appeared on the scene, he claimed to be a son of David.

The several claimants to be the messiah and descendants of David did not help the Jerusalem Nazoreans. As acknowledged descendants of David, the Nazoreans were most vulnerable. The constant threat of persecution needed only a spark to ignite it.

Persecution of Christians was going on all over the Empire. Pliny the Younger, governor of Bithynia, became alarmed at the number of persecutions and sent a letter to Emperor Trajan in 112: "Christians," he wrote, "did nothing improper or illegal. All they did was to rise up at dawn and sing hymns to Christ as a god, to repudiate adultery, murder, and similar disgraceful crimes, and in every way to conform to the law." This enlightened man was the nephew of Pliny the Elder, who had lost his life trying to help people escape from Pompeii.

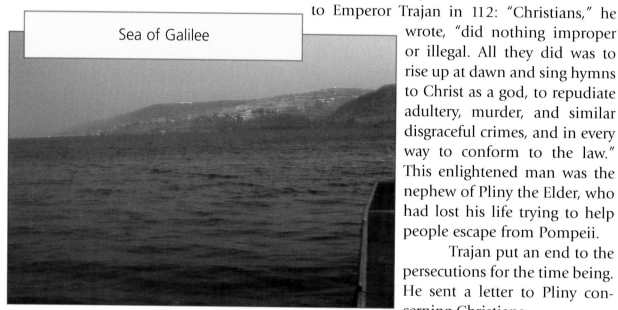

Sea of Galilee

Trajan put an end to the persecutions for the time being. He sent a letter to Pliny concerning Christians:

They are not to be sought out. If they are informed against and the charge is proved, they are to be punished, with this reservation—that if anyone denies that he is a Christian, and actually proves it, that is by worshipping our gods, he shall be pardoned as a result of his recantation, however suspect he may have been with respect to the past. Pamphlets published anonymously should carry no weight in any charge whatsoever. They constitute a very bad precedent and are also out of keeping with this age.

Revolts

Revolts by Jews in the Diaspora were frequent in these decades. In 115 a Jewish revolt in Egypt and Cyrenaica was vigorously put down by the Romans. Other disturbances broke out in Cyprus and in Mesopotamia. They were put down by Lucius Quietus, who later became governor of Judea, where he swiftly put an end to other rebellions there. This man had little regard for Jewish sensibilities. In 117 he erected the statue of Trajan in front of the altar of the destroyed Temple.

Division

Did persecution bring Jews and Nazoreans together? Or had they ever thought of themselves as separate? As has been mentioned, Jewish literature from this period gives no indication of a split between them prior to 135. Gamaliel II (in charge at Jamnia after 90) seems unaware of the existence of Christianity, although Samuel Hakatan (Samuel the Small One) was appointed to write the "Rakat Haminin" (the benediction on him who humbles those who have sinned). "Those who have sinned" may refer to those groups who operated outside the normative way of the Pharisees. They were called the *minima*, the sectarians. Possibly they included Sadducees, Gnostic groups, or Jewish Christians. But these special groups were hardly distinguishable from the other Jewish groups. Etienne Nodet suggests that it is only after 135 with Aquiba, who was a convert to Judaism from Christianity, that the eighteen benedictions excluded the Nazoreans.

Writings and Further Development of Christology

The Jamnian Pharisees had produced a canon of Scripture in 90, and a translation of the Pentateuch from the Septuagint was made by Aquila in 100. In these years, too, Christians were producing their own books, but the Pharisaic Jews seem to have been unaware of this.

The Gospel of John has traditionally been ascribed to John the son of Zebedee, who published it at Ephesus (Irenaeus, *Adversus Haereses*, 3:1, 1). Modern scholars attest, however, that the Gospel had a Johannine community of authors who used the testimony of "the disciple whom Jesus loved" (21:7) and produced it between the years 90 and 110. Scholars believe that an earlier document was used in its compilation, the "signs gospel." Countless details in the text show a familiarity with Palestine. There is a striking similarity between his Gospel and the nomenclature of the Dead Sea Scrolls: themes of light and darkness, and witness to the truth. James Charlesworth suggests that since the language is so similar there may have been some Essenes in John's community.

The writing of this Gospel coincides with the activities of those claiming to be the Jewish Messiah and claiming descent from David. John the evangelist not only presents Jesus as the Jewish Messiah but projects his existence to the beginning of creation:

> In the beginning was the Word, and the Word was with God, and the Word was God. He was in the beginning with God. All things came into being through him, and without him not one thing came into being. What has come into being in him was life, and the life was the light of all people. The light shines in the darkness, and the darkness did not overcome it. (John 1:1–5)

John's gospel greatly influenced the church's understanding of who Christ was. It would take another four hundred years to fully formulate it.

We learn from John of the many problems his community was having with the synagogue: "the Jews had already agreed that anyone who confessed Jesus to be the Messiah would be put out of the synagogue" (John 9:22).

Christian Jews had been expelled from the synagogue in Ephesus. We do not know how that affected our community on Mount Zion. They, of course, had their own synagogue.

Ever Mighty Rome

After Trajan's death in 117, Hadrian became emperor. Under this emperor, circumcision was forbidden. This does not seem to have been done as an outrage against the Jews. Castration was forbidden at the same time, and it seems that Hadrian did not distinguish the two. How widely this mandate was observed we do not know. Nonetheless it must have rankled the Jews. Spartianus, who wrote *The Life of Hadrian*, regarded it as a cause for the many rebellions. (Under the next emperor, Antoninus Pius, circumcision was permitted but castration continued to be forbidden.)

Hadrian, described as "fair-minded," was a man of varied genius who wrote poetry, sang, danced, organized his Empire, built walls, fought, and traveled. Justin Martyr, writing a century later, records that a provincial governor, Serennius Granianus, had written an appeal on behalf of Christians to Hadrian to end the popular clamor of sentencing them to death without trial. The emperor had replied that the governor "not pay attention to frivolous accusations but to treat all according to the rule of Law."

Hadrian in Jerusalem

In the year 130, Hadrian arrived personally in Jerusalem. Epiphanius, writing in 392, tells us:

> And he found the entire city crushed to the ground, the Temple of God demolished, except for a few homes and the small church of God where the returning disciples, after the Savior left them from the Mount of Olives, went up to the upper room. It had been built on the part of Sion

that was left over from the city, together with some dwellings and seven synagogues which remained on the mountain like cottages. Of these, a single one remained up to the time of Bishop Maximos and Emperor Constantinos like a shelter left in a vineyard. Scripture says "like a hut in a vineyard, like a shed in a melon patch." (Isaiah 1:8)

Doubtless the source for Epiphanius, who was a Palestinian by birth, was the Jewish Christians who still lived on Mount Zion in his day. By his time the ancient synagogue would have been called a church, a term which came into use only after 150.

Hadrian decided to rebuild the city and call it after himself, Aelia Capitolina (his family name was Aelius). The Temple was now dedicated to Jupiter. In Bethlehem a grove to Adonis was planted over the sacred grotto that Christians regarded as the birthplace of Jesus. We can only surmise how this affected the community on Mount Zion. Pilgrims such as Helena and Egeria, visiting in the fourth century after Christianity had become an accepted religion, were able to pinpoint places associated with Jesus, thus suggesting that they were never abandoned. Christians continued to pray at such places.

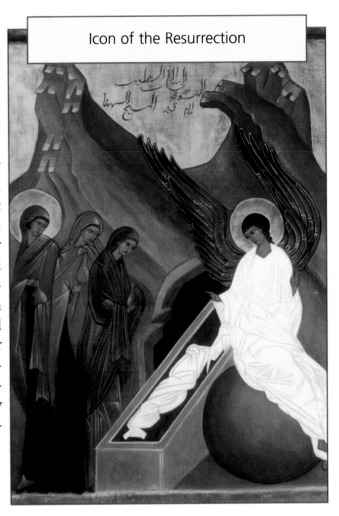

Icon of the Resurrection

The Bar Kokhba Rebellion

The rebellion of Bar Kokhba started in 134. Tineius Rufus was governor of Judea but he was overwhelmed by the rebels and was withdrawn and sent to Britain. Julius Severus took his place.

Simon Bar Kokhba ("son of a star") claimed to be the Messiah and to be a descendant of David. He had the full support of Rabbi Aquiba, leader of the Jamnian school. Aquiba is quoted in Rabbinic literature as having suggested the name Bar Kokhba for Simon as a Messianic description, based on the book of Numbers: "A star shall come out of Jacob and a scepter shall rise out of Israel" (24:17).

Aquiba later paid for this with crucifixion by the Romans.

The revolt at first met with some success through guerrilla tactics. Bar Kokhba was hailed as a hero and messiah. It is not certain that he ever entered Jerusalem. He was defeated at Batthera near Jerusalem. The Romans subdued the uprising, ruthlessly killing men, women, and children and appropriating their land.

Bar Kokhba's claims to be the Messiah were anathema to Christians. Justin Martyr tells us that Bar Kokhba himself had ordered the Christians to be sentenced to terrible punishment if they did not deny Jesus Christ and blaspheme him. Eusebius calls Bar Kokhba "a bloodthirsty bandit who on the strength of his name paraded himself as a luminary come down from heaven to shine upon their misery."

From 135 on, the Jewish race was forbidden to set foot anywhere in the neighborhood of Jerusalem under the ordinances of Hadrian, which ensured that "not even from a distance might Jews have a view of their ancestral soil" (Eusebius). Jerusalem was renamed Aelia Capitolina and the city was colonized by an "alien race." Statues of the Roman deities were set up in the temple and holy places and would remain there for almost three hundred years.

Were the Nazoreans Expelled?

Because the Nazoreans had not supported Bar Kokhba, it is possible that after the rebellion was put down, they were allowed to remain in Jerusalem. Or perhaps,

Mosaic in the church at Tabgha, traditional site of the multiplication of the loaves and fishes

when a much milder emperor, Antoninus Pius, succeeded Hadrian in 138, the Jewish Christians drifted back to Mount Zion.

Gentile Christians arrived in Jerusalem after 135. A gentile bishop, Marcus, was installed and resided at Caesarea.

Sulpicius Severus, writing three centuries later, says of this period:

> Because at that time the Christians from the Jews were very influential, the church in Jerusalem that came from the circumcision had a priest "Bishop." Hadrian ordered a military cohort to watch the entrance to Jerusalem to keep the Jews from entering. That again was an advantage for the Christian faith because at that time almost all that were under the law recognized Jesus as God, who had subjected himself to the law. Doubtless this was ordained by the Lord so that the service of the law would be substituted by the freedom of the faith and the church. So for the first time, Marcus, who came from the Gentiles, became Bishop of Jerusalem. Persecution came to an end. Hadrian thought it unjust that someone who had not committed any crime should be accused and found guilty. Under Antoninus Pius, his successor, the church did enjoy peace.

The bishops after the year 135 were gentile. The Jewish community continued to exist, but recognized the gentile bishops at Caesarea. They kept their own autonomy as Jewish believers in Christ.

EPILOGUE

From 135 CE, the bishops of Palestine were gentile, and the Jewish Christians came under the jurisdiction of the bishop at Caesarea.

In the first century, communities had developed along diverse lines, and these differences had been accepted. There had been deep disparity between Jewish Christians and Pauline Gentile Christians over observance of law and circumcision. These differences became more pronounced as the political situation changed. Dealing with heretics and excluding them came only after 150.

Jewish-Christian missionaries from Palestine were active in Alexandria at a very early date. Both Clement of Alexandria and Origen quote a Jewish-Christian Gospel according to the Hebrews. A tradition contained in the Pseudo-Clementine Homilies records that Barnabas, described as Hebrew and a staunch supporter of Peter and James, was the first missionary in Alexandria. Jewish Christians brought Christianity to Egypt. Jewish Christians were active at an early date in Carthage and in Rome, Asia Minor, and elsewhere.

After the Council of Caesarea (196 CE), we hear of Jewish-Christian opposition in Jerusalem against the bishops Narcissus and Alexander of Caesarea. By 220, we hear that the Nazoreans built a wall around Mount Zion in order to protect themselves against gentile influence. (Coins from this time have been found in the sills of the Essene gate.) When Eusebius visited Mount Zion in his youth (300 CE), he found the place very isolated and saw with his own eyes the area around the wall being plowed by veterans of the Roman legion.

In the year 333, a man known to us only as the Pilgrim of Bordeaux arrived in the Holy City. He too mentions the wall. According to his itinerary, he did not go as other pilgrims did to the Holy Sepulcher. Instead he took the road from the Temple to Mount Zion. He records for us how he came down from the Temple to the Siloam pool and ascended Mount Zion, passed the ruins of the house of Caiaphas, the high priest in the time of Jesus, and entered the "wall of Sion." He observed that a synagogue, still visible, was left standing on the site. He also exited through the "wall of Sion." Some scholars think he may have been a Jewish Christian. The synagogue he saw could only have been the Jewish-Christian one. The Bordeaux pilgrim also tells us that at that time, Jews were allowed in Jerusalem only once a year to lament the destruction of the Temple.

Up to the Council of Nicea (325 CE), a modus vivendi was observed between gentile and Jewish Christians. Their Jewish way of life and the autonomy of the

Nazoreans were accepted by the other Christians. Eusebius called them their "brothers who guarded the throne of James."

But after 325 there followed a very critical period. The Jewish Christians had not attended the Council and refused to accept the decisions of Nicea.

Their adherence to Jewish customs, especially circumcision and observance of Jewish holy days, naturally alienated them from the church of the gentiles, and with their refusal to accept the decisions of Nicea, Jewish Christians were cut off. They were ostracized; they were considered outsiders, even heretics. Around 337, under Bishop Maximos and Emperor Constantine, they seem to have been excommunicated. A low point of bigotry was reached by Jerome when he wrote: "The Nazoreans are neither Jews, because they believe in Christ, nor are they Christians, because they live Jewish lives."

At the turn of the fourth and fifth century, the few Nazoreans left on Mount Zion were gradually integrated into the imperial Orthodox Church. It is regrettable that the Jewish branch of Christianity vanished. Squeezed between the anvil of Rabbinic Judaism and the hammer of Byzantine Christianity, the Nazoreans never had a chance to survive, although according to the Pilgrim of Piacenza there were Jewish Christians in Nazareth when he visited in 570.

According to another pilgrim, Arculfus, some of the Jewish Christians apparently remained in Jerusalem until the second half of the seventh century. David Flusser contends that some even survived in Arabia until the tenth century.

It is sad to think that the generous Jews who had stretched out their hands to the gentiles through Peter and James during the Apostolic Council of Jerusalem were then cut off by the narrow-minded gentile Christians when Christianity became accepted in the Roman world. With the demise of the Jewish branch of Christianity, the church lost its cultural counterbalance to the structure of Hellenistic thought.

Casting a net on the Sea of Galilee

WORKS CITED

"Ascent of Isaiah," in *The Old Testament Pseudepigrapha*, edited by James H. Charlesworth. London: Darton, Longman and Todd, 1985.

Audet, Jean Paul. *La Didache, Instructions des Apotres*. Paris: Librairie Lecoffre, 1957.

Avalos, Hector. *Health Care and the Rise of Christianity*. Peabody, MA: Hendrickson Publishers, 1999.

Baron, Salo W. *A Social and Religious History of the Jews*. New York: Columbia University Press, 1952.

Bauckham, Richard. *Jude and the Relatives of Jesus in the Early Church*. Edinburgh: T and T Clark, 1990.

————. *The Book of Acts in Its Palestinian Setting*. Grand Rapids, MI: William B. Eerdmans, 1995.

Brown, Raymond. *The Birth of the Messiah*. New York: Doubleday, 1990.

————. *An Introduction to the New Testament*. New York: Doubleday, 1997.

Charlesworth, James H. *Critical Reflections on the Odes of Solomon*. Oxford: Clarendon Press, 1973.

————. *Jesus and the Dead Sea Scrolls*. New York: Crossroad, 1991.

Clapper, Brian. "Community of Goods in the Early Christian Church." In *Aufstieg und Niedergang der römischen Welt*, edited by W. Hasse and H. Temporini. 11, 26, 2 pp. 1730–1774.

————. "With the Oldest Monks." *Journal of Theological Studies* NS 49 (1998): 1–55.

Clement of Alexandria. *The Writings of Clement of Alexandria*. Edinburgh: T and T Clark, 1867.

Eisenman, Robert. *James the Brother of Jesus: The Key to Unlocking the Secrets of Early Christianity and the Dead Sea Scrolls*. New York: Viking Penguin, 1997.

Epiphanius of Salamis. *Panarion* and *De Mensuris et Ponderibus*.

Eusebius. *The History of the Church from Christ to Constantine*. New York: Dorset Press, 1965.

Flusser, David. *Jewish Sources in Early Christianity*. Jerusalem: MOD Books, 1996.

Fortna, Robert. *The Fourth Gospel and Its Predecessors*. Philadelphia: Fortress Press, 1988.

Foster, Paul. *The Writings of the Apostolic Fathers*. London: T and T Clark, 2007.

Frend, W.H.C. *The Rise of Christianity*. Philadelphia: Fortress Press, 1984.

Hall, Stuart, G., ed. *Melito of Sardis: On Pascha and Fragments*. Oxford: Oxford University Press, 1991.

Horbury, William. *Jewish Messianism and the Cult of Christ*. London: SCM Press Ltd., 1998.

Ignatius of Antioch. "Letters." In *The Apostolic Fathers*. London: Heinemann, 1912.

Irenaeus. "Adversus Haereses." In *Apostolic Fathers*. Peabody, MA: Hendrickson, 1994.

Jasper, R.C.D., and G.J. Cuming, translators. *Prayers of the Eucharist, Early and Reformed*. 3rd ed. Collegeville, MN: Liturgical Press, 1987.

Jeremias, Joachim. *Jerusalem at the Time of Jesus*. London: SCM Press Ltd., 1969.

Jerome. *De Viris Illustribus*. Patrologia Latina XXIII. Edited by J.-P. Migne. 217 vols. Paris 1844–1864.

Josephus, Flavius. *Complete Works*. Grand Rapids, MI: Kregel Publications, 1977.

Justin Martyr. "Apologia." In *Apostolic Fathers*. Peabody, MA: Hendrickson: 1994.

Kraft, Robert A., and George W.E. Nickelsburg, eds. *Early Judaism and Its Modern Interpreters*. Atlanta: Scholars Press, 1986.

Library of the Palestinian Pilgrims' Text Society. New York: AMS Press, 1971.

Manns, Frédéric. *Le récit de la Dormition de Marie* (Vatican grec 1982). Contribution à l'étude des origines de l'exégèse chrétienne. Jerusalem: Franciscan Printing Press, 1989.

Migne, J.-P., ed. Patrologia Latina II, III, IV. 217 vols. Paris 1844–1864.

Miller, Burrows. *The Dead Sea Scrolls*. New York: Viking Press, 1951.

Murphy O'Connor, Jerome. *Paul: A Critical Life*. Oxford: Clarendon Press, 1996.

Nauch, W. *Tradition and Character of Saint John*. Tübingen, 1957.

Nodet, Etienne, and J. Taylor. *The Origins of Christianity*. Minneapolis, MN: Liturgical Press, 1998.

Philo. *Works of Philo*. Peabody, MA: Hendrickson Publishers, 1993.

Riesner, Rainer. *Bethany Beyond the Jordan, Topography, Theology and History in the Fourth Gospel*. Tyndale New Testament lecture, 1986.

Riessler P. *Altjüdisches Schrifttum ausserhalb der Bibel*. Heidelberg, 1966.

Safrai, Shmuel, and M. Stern. *The Jewish People in the First Century: Historical Geography, Political History, Social, Cultural and Religious Life and Institutions*. Philadelphia: Fortress Press, 1975.

Schoedel, W.R. *Ignatius of Antioch*. Philadelphia: Fortress Press, 1985.

Suetonius. *The Lives of the Twelve Caesars*. Trans. J.C. Rolfe. Cambridge, MA: Harvard University Press, 1979.

Sulpicius Severus. *Sacred History*. Patrologia Latina XX. Edited by J.-P. Migne. 217 vols. Paris 1844–1864.

Tacitus. *The Complete Works*. New York: Modern Library, 1942.

Tarby, A. *La Prière eucharistique de l'église de Jérusalem*. Collection Théologie historique 17. Paris: Beauchesne, 1972.

Van de Sandt, Huub, and David Flusser. *The Didache: Its Jewish Source and Its Place in Early Judaism and Christianity.* Minneapolis: Fortress Press 2002.

Wuellner, Wilhelm. *The Meaning of Fishers of Men.* Philadelphia, PA: Westminster Press, 1981.